Let's Create!

Plastic
Cardboard
Fabrics
Clay

BARRON'S

Text and Exercices: Anna Olimós Plomer

All inquiries should be addressed to:
Barron's Educational Series, Inc.
250 Wireless Blvd.
Hauppauge, NY 11788
www.barronseduc.com

International Standard Book No. 0-7641-2571-0
Library of Congress Catalog Card No.: 00-101641

Printed in Spain
9 8 7 6 5 4 3 2 1

Contents

Plastic

Plastic

Plastic

Cardboard

Fabrics

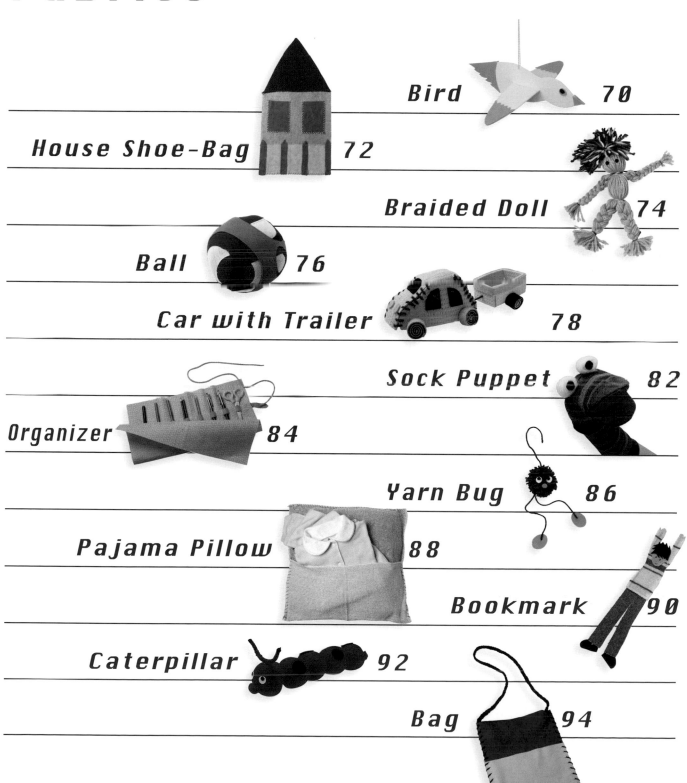

Clay

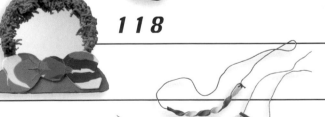

Introduction

Plastic

B ottles, ballpoint pens, boxes, balls, plates, bags, buttons…Look carefully around you and you will see an infinite number of plastic objects. Have you ever noticed that we use many things made of this material every day? If you pay close attention you will also notice that there are all kinds of plastics: hard, transparent, flexible, soft, colorful… Plastic is not a biodegradable material. This means that it must be recycled whenever possible, that is, reused, because if we just throw it away it is not good for the natural environment.

Did you know that with a little imagination plastic can be reused to make many fun things? Although it may seem difficult to do, it is not. All you need are some plastic objects that you have at home and a little bit of skill to work with them. In this book you will find a number of ingenious ideas for creating a whole lot of different things: a big monster to scare your friends, a doll for storing your things, a boat to float on the water, a hoop for playing basketball… You will see that it is possible to make all kinds of useful and entertaining objects with plastic bottles, plates, bags, and straws.

A few tools are necessary in order to make these projects. They can be easily found at home: scissors, staples, and transparent adhesive tape. Be sure to carefully follow the steps as they are shown. Sometimes some of the materials that we suggest can be substituted with something you like more, that way your creation can be more personal.

Cardboard

An endless array of items made of cardboard, like corrugated boxes, toilet tissue or paper towel tubes, shoeboxes, and much more, confirm the fact that cardboard is a common material. It is made from pulp or sometimes from bonding together a number of layered sheets of paper. This familiar material comes in various thicknesses and sizes: thin, heavy, wavy, smooth. If you look around your house, you will find these types of cardboard in the form of boxes or tubes. Also, they are very often used for packing or as wrapping material for other objects, in which case they are discarded once they have fulfilled their function. Don't throw them away! They can be important parts of your craft projects.

This book presents a great number of ideas for making many different craft projects from cardboard sheets and objects. You will find Ping-Pong paddles for playing with your friends, flip-flops that can be part of a costume, a parking garage to park your cars, and a coin bank doll to save your money. All these craft projects are fun and easy to make; you only need the cardboard objects that you find around your house and a little patience and imagination. Let's explore the many possibilities that cardboard offers and have fun creating with it!

Although cardboard comes in many colors, you will notice that here we have chosen to use brown cardboard. This will allow you to paint it with the colors that you like best, and thus make your projects more personal and creative. To make these projects you will need to have some basic tools that are easily found at home (scissors, staples, glue...) and then follow the steps carefully.

Fabrics

Look around carefully and you will see that fabrics are a part of almost every area of our daily lives. The art of weaving is very old. It basically consists of interweaving several pieces of thread alternately and regularly until a solid sheet or panel has been created. In the old days, only natural fibers were used. But now an infinite number of artificial or synthetic fabrics (fabrics made from materials not found in nature, like nylon) are also used.

As you will notice, fabrics are a common thing in our daily lives. You can create new and original objects from different types of fabrics. To make the craft projects that we show here you will not have to cut up dresses and outfits. You will find remnants, old clothing, yarn, cleaning cloths, old rags, socks and other things to make the projects. See for yourself how you will be able to make a variety of things with this material that are fun and that will be useful at the same time: a pillow to hide your pajamas, a beautiful braided doll, an organizer for pens and pencils, or a sock puppet to amuse your friends with.

Commonly found natural and synthetic fabrics have been used to make the crafts listed in this book, which are easy to manipulate due to their inherent characteristics. Some of the projects will serve as a very basic introduction to the world of sewing. All you need is a large size needle and a little skill to work it through the structure of the fabric.

In order to make these craft projects, you will need to have a number of tools that you should be able to find at home (scissors, large size needle, glue) and you will have to follow the steps carefully. Also, you will find that you can achieve different results by making slight changes. We suggest some ideas to help you do so.

Clay

Red, green, orange…modeling clay is a plastic material that is found in various colors and that is used basically for making shapes. It offers a great variety of uses in the craft world, and with it we can create decorative shapes and useful and original objects.

You will find in this book different ideas for making things with modeling clay: coasters, figures to decorate your clothes hangers, decorative tops for your pencils, necklaces, magnets, and more. You can make all of them with modeling clay and a few simple tools. Throughout this book you will learn different ways of working with this material, such as extruding it, rolling it, mixing colors, and combining layers of different colors. In addition, you will be introduced to some tools used to apply better finishes to your creations.

In some of the projects shown in the book we use a rolling pin to flatten the modeling clay to make thin sheets. If you do not have one, a bottle, a can or any other heavy cylindrical object will serve the same purpose. You will also discover that commonly used objects, such as a strainer, can be useful to model the clay and to mold new shapes that will make your projects more attractive. You will notice that we varnish only the projects that require varnish to increase their

durability or to prevent them from staining. Even so, if you wish, you can varnish any object that you make out of modeling clay.

In order to do the projects all you need is to have modeling clay of various colors and a few tools that you will find in your school or in your home (plastic knife, awl, rolling pin…) and to follow the steps carefully.

We suggest ideas at the end of these projects that can be slightly changed to get different results.

As you can see, you can make a number of great products with few materials.

Let's get to work!

Let's Create!

Plastic

Bubble Monster

Bubble plastic is good for more than wrapping things. With a little imagination you can create this friendly bubble monster. Follow these steps carefully.

1 Draw and cut out the outline of the monster on the piece of yellow cardboard.

2 Cut two pieces of bubble wrap and draw the outline on both, using the poster board as a guide. Keep in mind that for both pieces to be identical you will have to trace one on the bubble side and the other on the smooth side of the plastic. Then cut them out.

3 Staple both monster cut-outs to each other on the smooth sides. Staple only along the body, leaving unstapled the legs, part of the tail and the 4 in. (10 cm) that you must leave for the mouth.

Toolbox

You will need:
- scissors
- black permanent marker
- stapler
- transparent tape
- a piece of green bubble plastic wrapping 60 × 14 in. (150 × 35 cm)
- a red, matte plastic divider
- small white plastic cups (at least 2)
- a sheet of white contact paper
- a sheet of yellow poster board

4 Draw 2 circles on the sheet of contact paper with the black permanent marker and cut them out. Attach them to the end of the snout to make the nose.

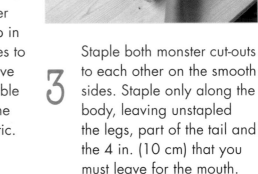

14

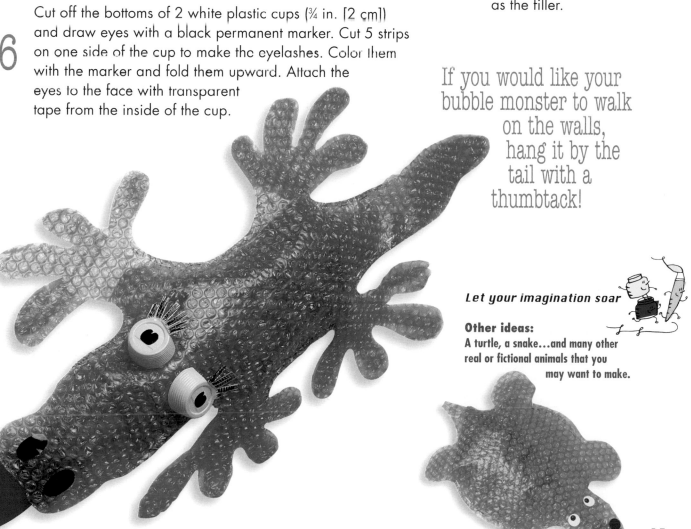

5 To make the tongue, cut a 5½ in. (14 cm) strip from the red divider and attach it to the inside of the mouth with transparent tape.

6 Cut off the bottoms of 2 white plastic cups (¾ in. [2 cm]) and draw eyes with a black permanent marker. Cut 5 strips on one side of the cup to make the eyelashes. Color them with the marker and fold them upward. Attach the eyes to the face with transparent tape from the inside of the cup.

7 Insert the scraps of the green plastic leftover from cutting the shapes into the monster's mouth. It will act as the filler.

If you would like your bubble monster to walk on the walls, hang it by the tail with a thumbtack!

Let your imagination soar

Other ideas:
A turtle, a snake...and many other real or fictional animals that you may want to make.

15

Sun Clock

Would you like to make a fun wall clock and to learn how to tell time with it? To create your sun clock follow these instructions.

Toolbox

You will need:
- scissors
- hole puncher
- permanent markers, one black and one red
- transparent tape
- 12 round white stickers
- 3 large plastic plates (2 green and 1 yellow)
- orange gift wrapping ribbon
- a paper clasp
- sheets of red and white contact paper

1. Draw sun rays around the back of a yellow plate with a black permanent marker (remember that you have to make 12 sun rays, as many as hours on a clock). Then cut them out.

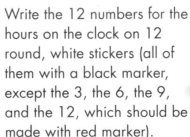

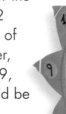

2. Draw two circles on the back of a sheet of white contact paper and cut them out. Paint 2 large dots on them with the black permanent marker to make the eyes of the sun clock. Then draw a mouth on the back of a sheet of red contact paper and cut it out.

3. Write the 12 numbers for the hours on the clock on 12 round, white stickers (all of them with a black marker, except the 3, the 6, the 9, and the 12, which should be made with red marker).

4. Now place each round sticker on the sun rays following the order of the hours on a clock. Attach the mouth and the eyes, and draw eyebrows over them with a black permanent marker. Leave enough space between the mouth and the eyes to fit the hands of the clock.

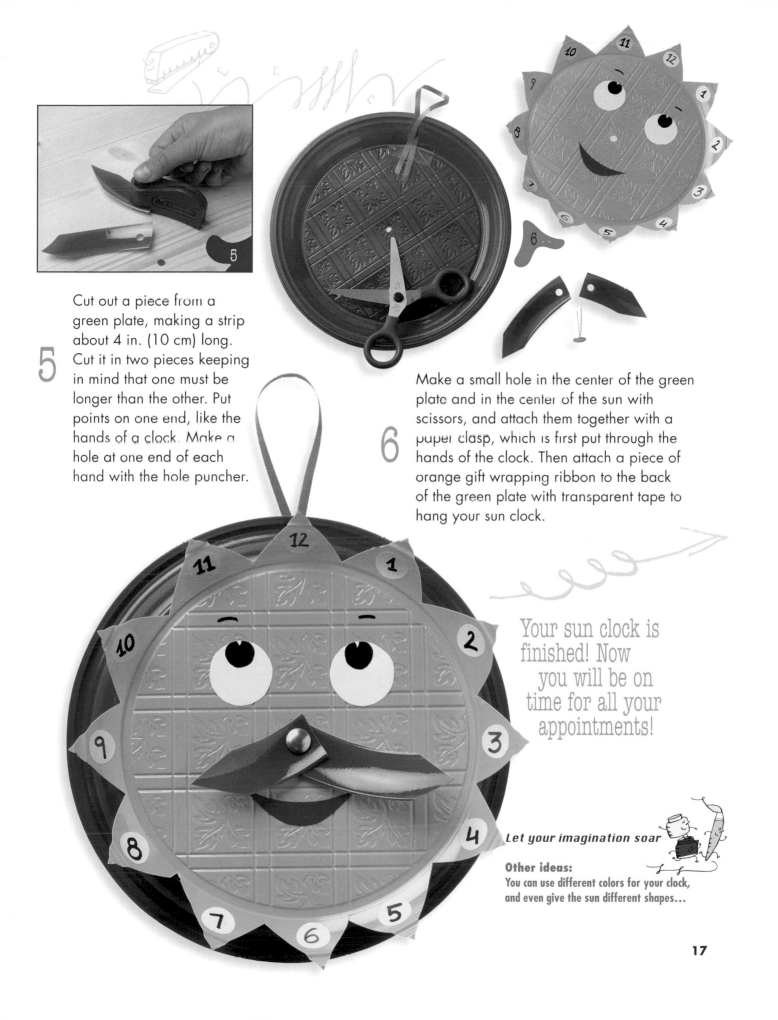

5 Cut out a piece from a green plate, making a strip about 4 in. (10 cm) long. Cut it in two pieces keeping in mind that one must be longer than the other. Put points on one end, like the hands of a clock. Make a hole at one end of each hand with the hole puncher.

6 Make a small hole in the center of the green plate and in the center of the sun with scissors, and attach them together with a paper clasp, which is first put through the hands of the clock. Then attach a piece of orange gift wrapping ribbon to the back of the green plate with transparent tape to hang your sun clock.

Your sun clock is finished! Now you will be on time for all your appointments!

Let your imagination soar

Other ideas:
You can use different colors for your clock, and even give the sun different shapes...

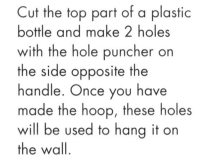

Basketball Hoop

Have fun and surprise your friends by making this original basketball hoop. Follow these steps carefully.

Toolbox

You will need:
- scissors
- hole puncher
- green, red, and black synthetic raffia
- red, black, and white tape
- a 39 in. (1 m) long piece of gray plastic wire
- a one gallon (5 liter) plastic bottle (with a side handle)
- an 18 × 18 in. (46 × 46 cm) Styrofoam sheet
- an 18 × 18 in. (46 × 46 cm) sheet of white contact paper

1 Cut the top part of a plastic bottle and make 2 holes with the hole puncher on the side opposite the handle. Once you have made the hoop, these holes will be used to hang it on the wall.

2 Cut out an 18 × 18 in. (46 × 46 cm) sheet of Styrofoam. Then cover it with the sheet of white contact paper and you will have the backboard for the basketball hoop.

3 Frame the board with red tape and then form an 8 × 8 in. (21 × 21 cm) square with black tape. Make a hole the size of the neck of the plastic bottle exactly in the middle and below one of the sides of this square. Use scissors for this.

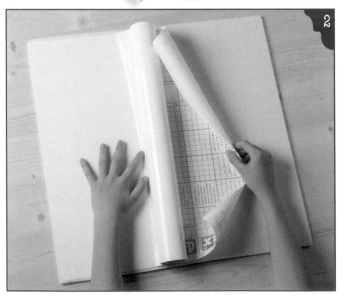

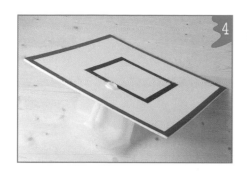

4 Insert the neck of the bottle through this hole. (If you wish you can wrap the mouth of the bottle where it sticks out with white tape to make sure it stays on the board).

Now insert the plastic wire through the neck of the bottle so that both ends cross each other in the back. Attach them to the bottle with red tape and you will have made the basketball hoop.

6

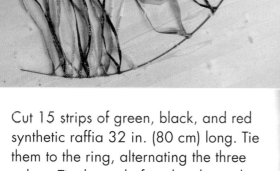

Cut 15 strips of green, black, and red synthetic raffia 32 in. (80 cm) long. Tie them to the ring, alternating the three colors. Tie the end of each color to the one next to it (which will be a different color) about 5 in. (12 cm) below the ring. Repeat this step to create the net.

5

Would you like to use it as a score board? Write the points with a non-permanent black marker, and you will be able to erase them and do it again and again.

Let your imagination soar

Other ideas:
You can change the shape of the board and the colors...

Chick Puzzle

Design your own puzzle and then show how you can solve it. To make it, follow these instructions.

Toolbox

You will need:
- scissors
- white, red, green, yellow, and transparent contact paper
- permanent black marker
- a sheet of purple paper 8½ × 11 in. (DIN-A4)

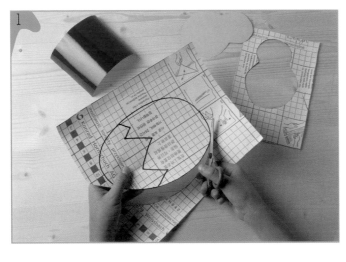

1. Draw the cracked egg, the chick's body, the wing, the beak, and the grass on the back of the sheets of contact paper (for each drawing you must use the corresponding colored sheets). Then cut out each piece.

2. Attach the body and the beak of the chick to the middle of the purple sheet of paper and draw the eyes with a permanent black marker.

3. Then glue the rest of the pieces of the composition: first attach the two parts of the egg (one above the chick and the other below), then the wing, and finally the grass covering the base of the egg.

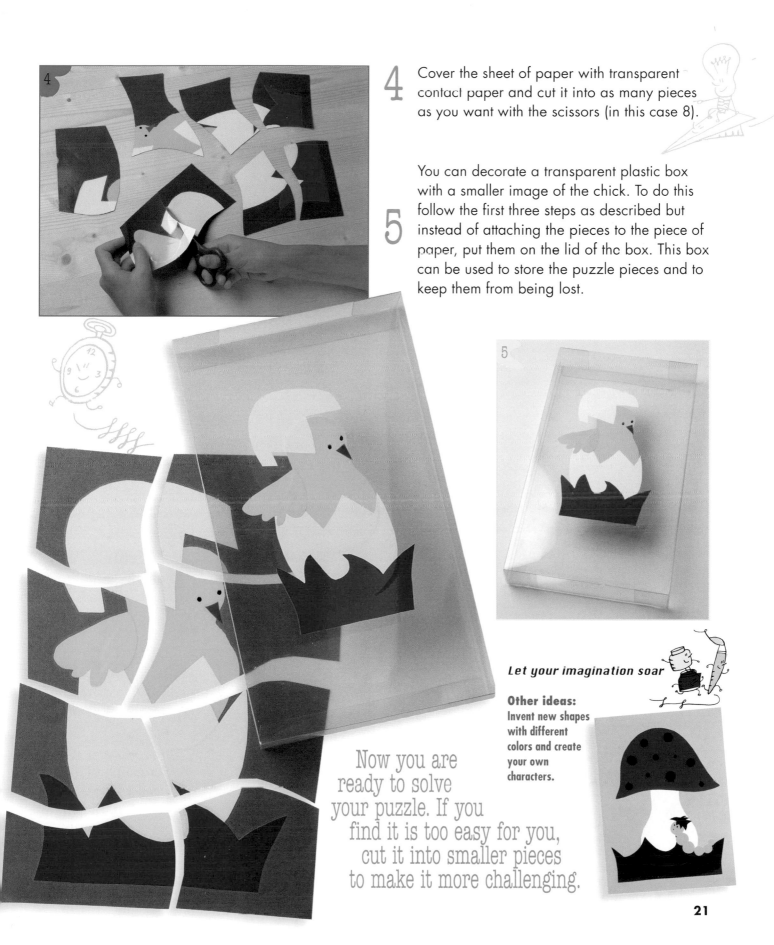

4 Cover the sheet of paper with transparent contact paper and cut it into as many pieces as you want with the scissors (in this case 8).

5 You can decorate a transparent plastic box with a smaller image of the chick. To do this follow the first three steps as described but instead of attaching the pieces to the piece of paper, put them on the lid of the box. This box can be used to store the puzzle pieces and to keep them from being lost.

Now you are ready to solve your puzzle. If you find it is too easy for you, cut it into smaller pieces to make it more challenging.

Let your imagination soar

Other ideas:
Invent new shapes with different colors and create your own characters.

Dancing Puppet

He can walk, dance, jump...Bring to life a puppet created by you! To do so, follow these steps carefully.

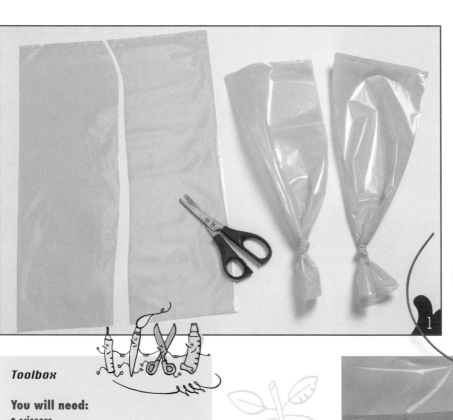

1 Cut the 2 bags in half lengthwise, so that you will have 4 strips of the same size. Tie knots at the open ends of two of the strips to make the arms.

Toolbox

You will need:
- scissors
- a long, thin paintbrush
- two permanent markers, one red and one black
- yellow and transparent tape
- 6 plastic cups (2 blue and 4 green)
- green round plastic string
- one Styrofoam ball
- 2 drinking straws
- 2 yellow plastic bags
  1½ × 10 in.
  (4 × 26 cm)

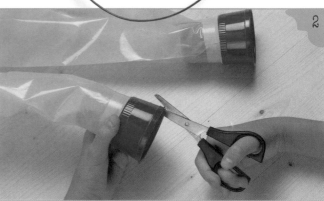

Attach the other 2 strips to green plastic cups with yellow tape. The cups will be the shoes and the strips two long yellow legs. Make two slits on the sides of the shoes, which later will be used to attach the strings for the puppet.

2

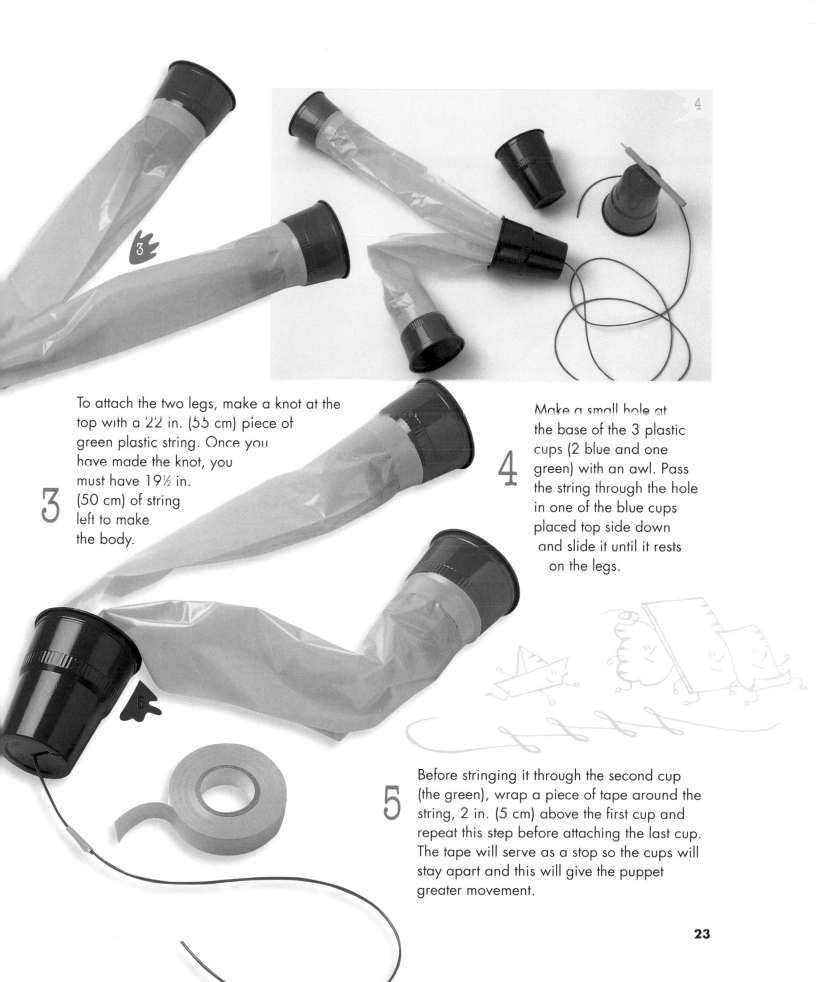

To attach the two legs, make a knot at the top with a 22 in. (55 cm) piece of green plastic string. Once you have made the knot, you must have 19½ in. (50 cm) of string left to make the body.

3

4 Make a small hole at the base of the 3 plastic cups (2 blue and one green) with an awl. Pass the string through the hole in one of the blue cups placed top side down and slide it until it rests on the legs.

5 Before stringing it through the second cup (the green), wrap a piece of tape around the string, 2 in. (5 cm) above the first cup and repeat this step before attaching the last cup. The tape will serve as a stop so the cups will stay apart and this will give the puppet greater movement.

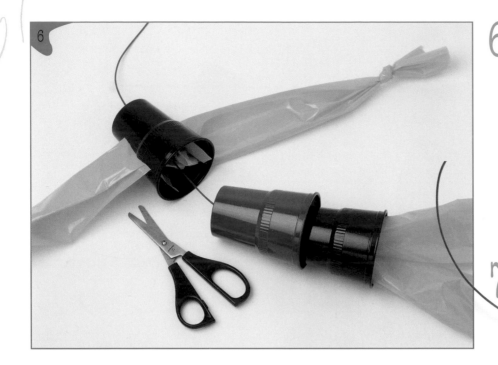

6 Make two 1¼ in. (3 cm) slits with the scissors on the sides of the last cup. Push the ends of the arms that do not have knots through them.

7 Pierce through the Styrofoam ball with the handle of a small brush. Draw the eyes and the nose with a black permanent marker, and the mouth with the red one. Pass the string through the ball until it reaches the body.

8 Make a hole in the remaining green cup and pass the string through it until it rests on the head as a hat. Cut two 36 in. (90 cm) pieces of green string and another 2 pieces 19½ in. (50 cm) long. Insert both long pieces into the cuts that you have previously made in the shoes and attach them on the inside with tape. Then make 2 small holes with the scissors on the hands of the puppet and pass the other two pieces of knotted string through them.

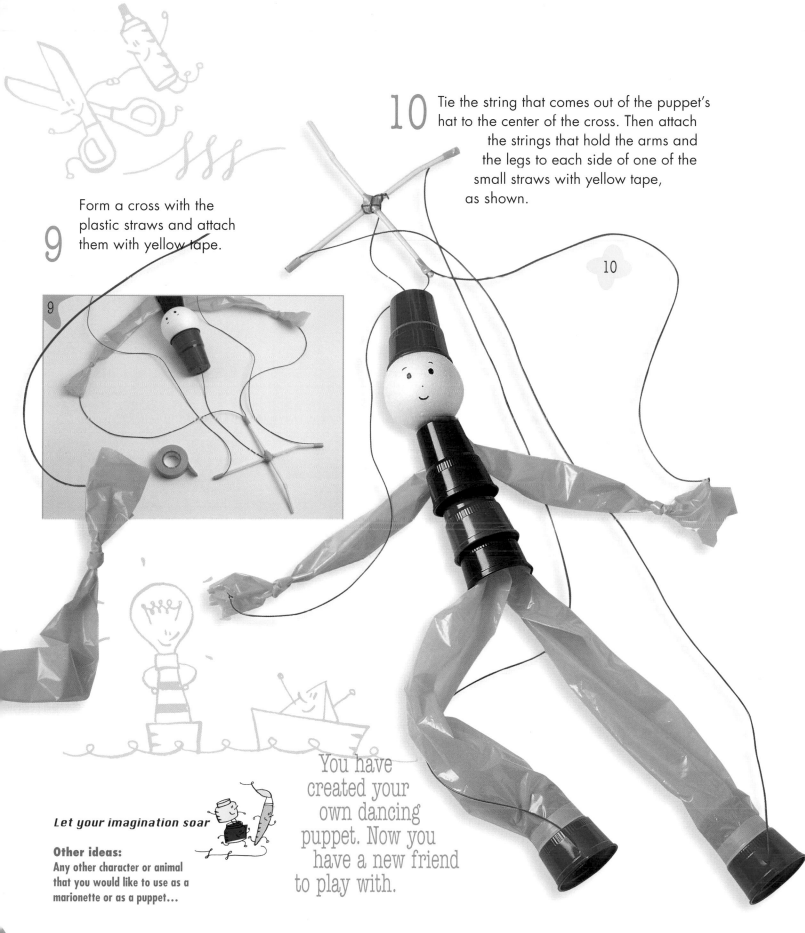

10 Tie the string that comes out of the puppet's hat to the center of the cross. Then attach the strings that hold the arms and the legs to each side of one of the small straws with yellow tape, as shown.

9 Form a cross with the plastic straws and attach them with yellow tape.

You have created your own dancing puppet. Now you have a new friend to play with.

Let your imagination soar

Other ideas:
Any other character or animal that you would like to use as a marionette or as a puppet...

Colorful Flowers

If you want to decorate a corner of your house or give flowers to someone special, create them yourself. Simply follow the step-by-step instructions.

1 Cut a blue plate into 4 equal parts but not all the way to the center (leave approximately ⅜ in. [1 cm]). Then cut off the edges.

2 Cut a square in the center of the plate by cutting three sides, leaving it attached on one of its sides. You will end up with a tab that you will have to fold down. Shape the four parts of the plate with scissors to make them resemble petals.

3 Place a round yellow sticker in the center of the flower, covering the hole, and another (green) star-shaped sticker over it.

4 Repeat steps 1 and 2 with a green plate, but this time, instead of rounding off the petals, cut shapes that resemble leaves.

5 Using the tab, attach the flower to the top of a plastic straw (where it bends) with green tape. Then add the leaves, sliding them up from the bottom end of the straw and attaching them in the middle.

Let your imagination soar

Other ideas:
You can make stars or flowers and leaves in a thousand shapes...

Now you have your first flower. Combine different colors and your bouquet will be more lively!

27

Backpack
Backpack
Backpack

Backpack

You can make a very original backpack to carry books to school or to take on a field trip. Follow these instructions and you will amaze everyone.

1 Cut off one of the bottles 6½ in. (16 cm) above the base (keep in mind that you will only use the part of the container that will be the body of your backpack). Cut off another bottle 2 in. (5 cm) above the base. You will use this part as the lid.

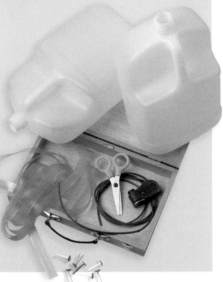

2 Make holes with the hole puncher at ⅜ in. (1 cm) below the edge of the backpack's body, spaced ¾ in. (2 cm) apart.

3 Wrap the green plastic string through the holes in such a way that the edge will look finished.

4 Cut 2 18 in. (45 cm) long pieces of the yellow plastic strips and another one 4 in. (10 cm) long. Make a notch in one end of the short piece and round off the other end using scissors.

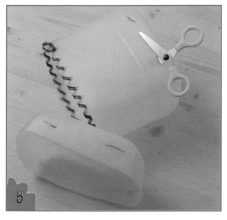

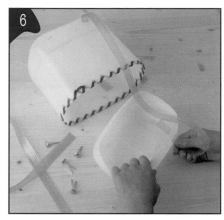

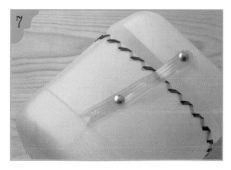

5 Cut two slits on one of the wide sides of the backpack's body (near the top), 4 inches (10 cm) apart. Also cut a slit in the center of the opposite side. Then make 2 holes in the lower part of the backpack and another one in the center of the opposite side. Ask an adult to help you.

6 You have to insert the 4 ends of the 2 long yellow strips through the holes that you have made in the bottle and fasten them with the 4 clasps to attach the lid to the body of the backpack through the slits.

7 Insert a clasp through the hole in the front part of the backpack's body. This will act as a button fastener. Attach the short yellow strap to the lid with another clasp. It will be easy for you to close the backpack.

Now you have a backpack. Fill it up, strap it to your back, and you are ready to show it off!

Let your imagination soar

Other ideas:
You can create other backpacks with bottles of different shapes and sizes. You can also decorate them with stickers...

Binoculars

Would you like to be an explorer? Would you like to see the world in blue? If you follow these steps, your binoculars will be a success.

1 Cut off the bottoms of the 2 bottles with the help of an adult. Paint them with white acrylic paint and then with orange. Paint the neck of the bottle blue.

2 Trace the bases of the 2 bottles on the cellophane with the permanent marker. Cut them out leaving an additional ⅜ in. (1 cm) around it. Cut this border so that it will have tabs all around.

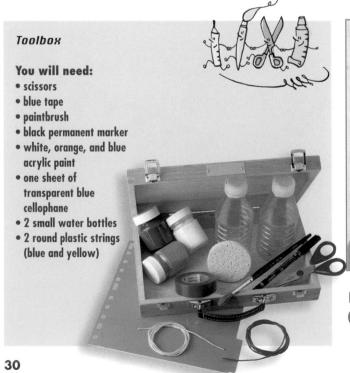

Toolbox

You will need:
- scissors
- blue tape
- paintbrush
- black permanent marker
- white, orange, and blue acrylic paint
- one sheet of transparent blue cellophane
- 2 small water bottles
- 2 round plastic strings (blue and yellow)

3 Place both circles in the bottoms of the bottles with the tabs to the outside and attach them with blue tape.

4 Then place the bottles side by side and attach them to each other with blue tape.

5 Cut one piece of blue plastic string and another yellow 39 in. (1 m) long. Twist them together and attach them to the sides of the binoculars with a piece of blue tape over the tape that is holding the bottles together.

You are ready to look at the world through your binoculars. See how many things you can discover!

Let your imagination soar

Other ideas:
Binoculars made with larger bottles, or a telescope...

A Thousand Faces

Would you like to have fun by changing the expressions on a face that you have created? To make this changing face, follow the steps carefully.

1   Draw the outline of a head on a 16 × 24 in. (40 × 60 cm) Styrofoam sheet and cut it out.

2   Cut 6 pieces of double-sided Velcro. Attach them to the place that corresponds to the forehead, the eyes, the nose, the mouth, and the neck. Then paint the face and the neck with flesh-colored acrylic paint and the shoulder area with stripes of different colors, to resemble a T-shirt.

3   Draw 3 pairs of eyes with a black permanent marker on a white divider. Also draw 3 different mouths and 3 different noses on a red divider and then cut out all the pieces.

Toolbox

You will need:
- scissors
- paintbrush
- a sheet of Styrofoam (16 × 24 in. [40 × 60 cm])
- acrylic paint of various colors
- a double-sided narrow strip of Velcro
- opaque plastic separators of various colors
- black permanent marker

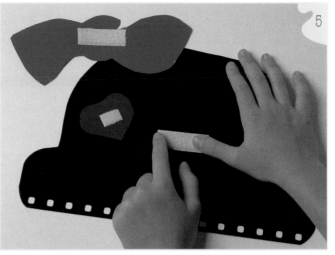

4 As in step 3, create different hair styles and hats, as well us u ile und bow ties that you can decorate as you wish with a black permanent marker. Use the colors that you like best for this.

5 Once you have cut out all the pieces, attach the other pieces of the double-sided Velcro to their back sides.

Let your imagination soar

Other ideas:
By changing the different pieces you can create a thousand different faces. Try to make the most original one!

You only have to choose some eyes, a nose, the hair, a mouth, and an accessory for the neck and attach them to the head.

Pencil Holder Doll

Would you like to keep your pencils in an original container? How about a doll to hold them? You can create it with a plastic bottle! Follow these steps and you will find it very easy.

2 Paint the eyes, the nose, the mouth, and the cheeks. Attach the orange cellophane grass to the head of the figure (as if it were a tiara) with yellow tape.

1 Insert a pencil in a Styrofoam ball and paint it with flesh-colored acrylic paint.

3 Fill the plastic bottle with gravel (only halfway).

Toolbox

You will need:
- scissors
- paintbrush
- yellow and blue tape
- 2 blue bags and one 1½ × 10 in. (4 × 26 cm) yellow bag
- one Styrofoam ball
- white, red, green, and flesh-colored acrylic paint
- one pencil of any color
- one 48 oz. (1.5 liter) water bottle
- orange cellophane grass
- gravel

4 Fold a blue bag to make a long strip. Attach it to the top end of the plastic bottle with transparent tape to make the arms.

5 Cut another blue bag in the shape of a rectangle and make two holes about 2 in. (5 cm) apart with the scissors. Insert the arms through them and dress the bottle as if it were a jacket. Attach it to the back of the bottle with transparent tape and wrap it at the neck with blue tape.

6 To make the pockets for the pencils, cut off the bottom of a yellow bag and insert the bottle through. Use blue tape to close the bottom of the pocket. Also tape the sides of the pockets to the sides of the bottle.

Now all you have to do is insert the head into the neck of the bottle and your doll will be finished. Your pencils are in good hands.

Let your imagination soar

Other ideas:
You can add pockets to your pencil holder doll with plastic adhesive tape and bags of different colors.

Spiders on a String

A simple plastic cup can be turned into a fun, long-legged spider. Do you dare? Just follow these steps.

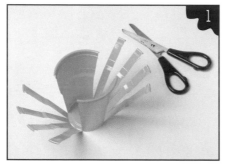

1. Cut the yellow cup from the rim to the base in such a way that you will have 4 – ⅜ in. (1 cm) wide strips. Parallel to these, cut 4 more strips of the same width on the opposite side.

2. Then cut off one uncut side of the cup at the base, and cut away the other side leaving two square tabs.

3. To shape the legs, fold all 8 strips in half. Round the two tabs with scissors to make the eyes.

4. Make two black dots on two green stickers with a permanent marker and stick them on the rounded tabs that you have made.

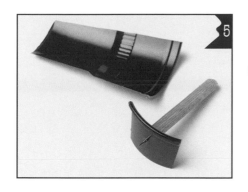

5 To make the mouths, use the scraps from the cups of the other spiders. Cut each one of them the same width as its base, and make a hole in the middle with an awl.

6 Insert a length of green plastic string through the holes made in the spider's mouth and body. Attach the mouth to the body with a piece of transparent tape.

These spiders can now live in any corner of your bedroom.

Let your imagination soar

Other ideas:
Different animals and different colors, for example, a butterfly, a fly...

Hang them from the ceiling and let them make their web.

37

Boat Boat Boat Boat

Boat

Embark on the adventure of making your own boat and become an expert captain. Navigate these steps to make your boat.

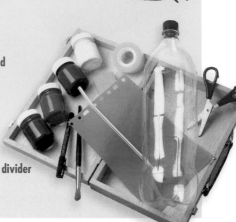

1 Cut a ½ gallon (2 liter) bottle in half, lengthwise, keeping the base and the neck. Draw designs on the outside with a black permanent marker.

2 Color these bands on the inside of the bottle with acrylic paints of different colors (green, blue, white, and orange).

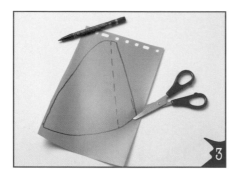

3 Draw a sail with a tab on a piece of green plastic divider and cut it out.

4 Fold the tab and attach it to the sail with transparent tape. Then insert a small drinking straw into it.

38

5 Push the mast with the sail into a piece of yellow modeling clay. Then place the mast in the middle of the boat.

Let your imagination sail and enjoy your boat!

Let your imagination soar

Other ideas:
You can change the colors and the decorations of your boat. You can also create a sailor with a piece of plastic the same way you made the bottle.

Cardboard

Ping-Pong Paddle

There's no need to buy paddles to play Ping-Pong. You can make them yourself by following these steps.

1 Draw and cut out two Ping-Pong paddles on a piece of flat, thick cardboard.

2 Using one of the cut out paddles as a pattern, draw and cut out two circles and two handles. The cut out circles should have flat bases.

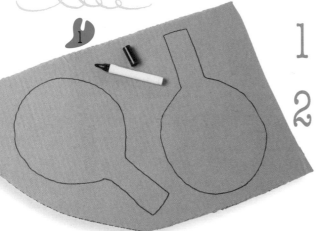

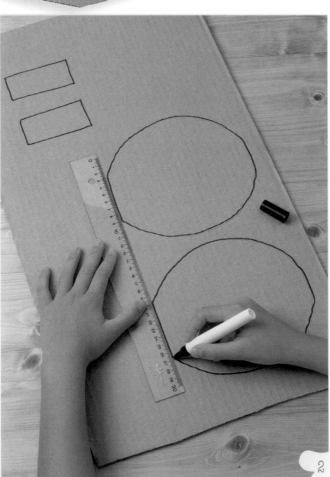

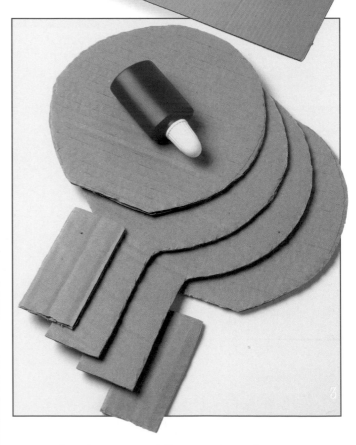

3 Glue the two paddles together. Then attach the circles and the two handles to each side of the paddle with glue.

42

4 Wrap the handle with black tape and paint both circles white.

5 When the white paint is dry, paint it pink using a foam pad.

Here is your paddle! Now you can play a great game of Ping-Pong!

Let your imagination soar

Other ideas:
You can create original paddles with different shapes, for example, a hand.

Snail

It is very easy to make a snail with two strips of cardboard. To bring it to life follow these step-by-step instructions.

You will need:
- thin, corrugated cardboard
- thin, smooth cardboard
- scissors and clothespins
- glue
- orange, green, white, blue, and red paint
- paintbrush
- marker

1 Draw the body of the snail on a thin, smooth piece of cardboard and cut it out.

2 Cut out a strip of thin, corrugated cardboard about 6 in. (15 cm) long and 1¼ in. (3 cm) wide, and paint orange stripes on it. This will be the shell of your snail.

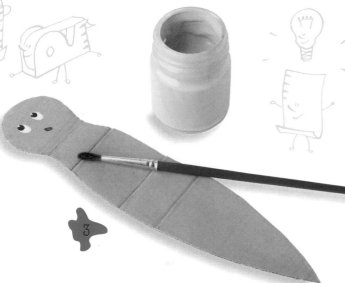

3 Paint the body green, and when it dries paint the eyes and the mouth of the snail.

4 Glue one of the ends of the strip to the body to make the shell. Roll it and hold it in place for a while using two clothespins. This way, when you let it go it will keep its spiral shape.

5 Cut out two strips of approximately 1½ in. (4 cm) long and ¼ in. (0.5 cm) wide from a piece of thin, corrugated cardboard to form the antennae.

You have finished your new pet! Put it in your room as a decoration.

Let your imagination soar

Other ideas:
Invent other pets that you can make with only two strips of cardboard, like a worm, a snake...

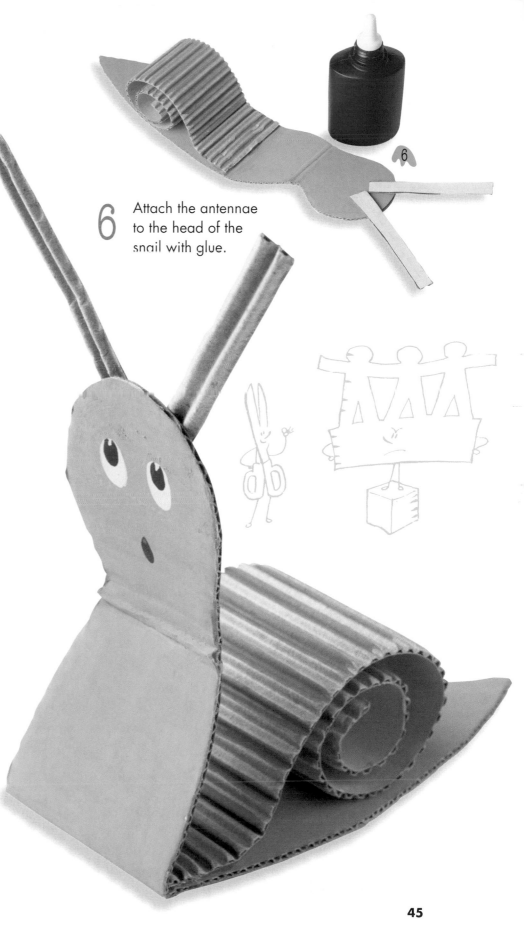

6 Attach the antennae to the head of the snail with glue.

Parking Garage

If you want your cars to be parked better than ever, make a sturdy parking garage by following these steps.

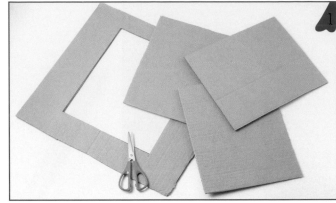

1   Draw and cut out 3 rectangles of about 12 × 10 in. (30 × 25 cm) on a piece of plain, thick cardboard.

2   Make a cut about 8 in. (20 cm) long at 1½ in. (4 cm) in from the *short* side of one of the rectangles. Repeat the procedure, but this time on the *long* side of another rectangle. These cuts will make the ramps.

Toolbox

You will need:
- thin, corrugated cardboard
- thick, smooth cardboard
- 6 toilet tissue tubes
- yellow tape
- scissors
- glue
- pink and gray paint
- paintbrush
- marker

3   Using the rectangle that does not have a ramp as a base, make the two levels of the parking garage using 3 toilet tissue tubes as columns on each level, and attach them to the rectangles with glue.

4   Finish the edges of the first and second levels with strips of thin corrugated cardboard about ¾ in. (2 cm) wide.

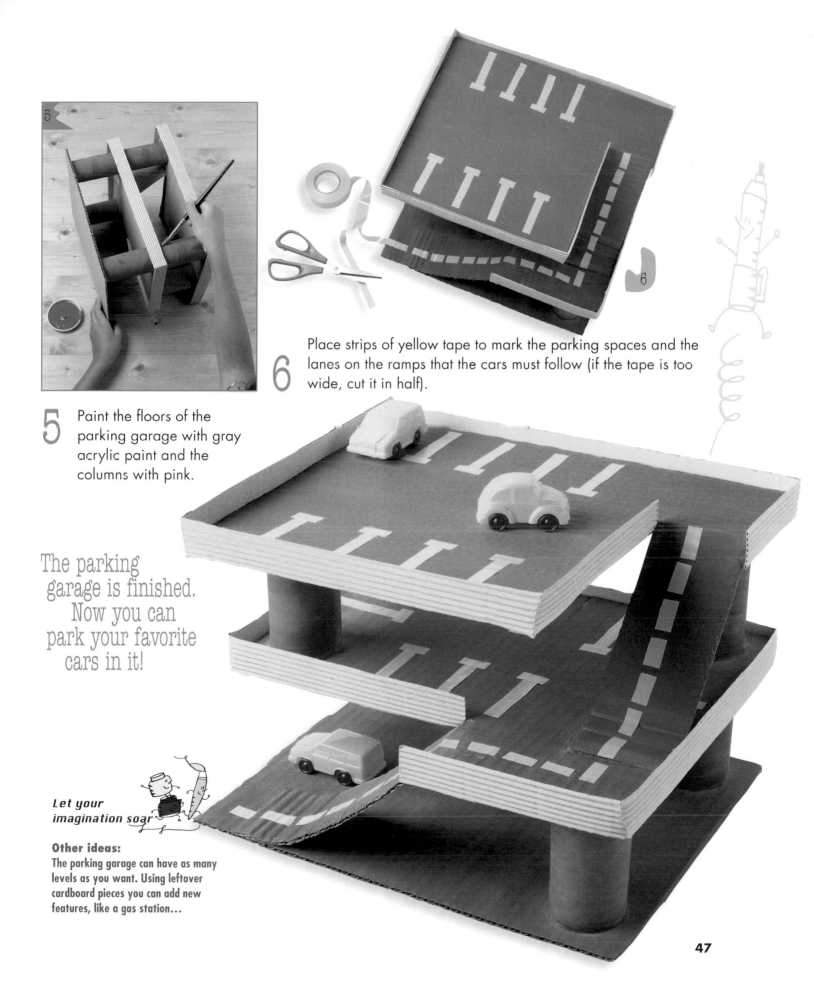

Place strips of yellow tape to mark the parking spaces and the lanes on the ramps that the cars must follow (if the tape is too wide, cut it in half).

6

5 Paint the floors of the parking garage with gray acrylic paint and the columns with pink.

The parking garage is finished. Now you can park your favorite cars in it!

Let your imagination soar

Other ideas:
The parking garage can have as many levels as you want. Using leftover cardboard pieces you can add new features, like a gas station...

Flip-Flops
Flip-Flops
Flip-Flops

Flip-Flops

Do you think you can make a pair of flip-flops? Follow these steps carefully and you will see how easy it is.

You will need:
- smooth, thick cardboard
- thin, corrugated cardboard
- scissors
- glue
- stapler
- white, red, and green paint
- paintbrush
- marker

1 Trace an outline of the shoe three times on a piece of smooth cardboard. Cut them out.

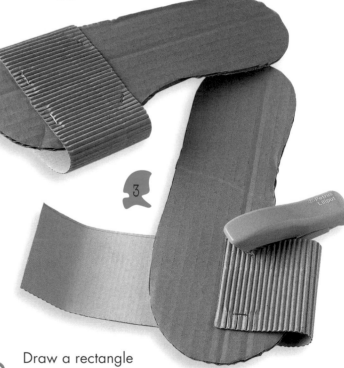

2 Draw a rectangle about 4 in. (10 cm) long by 2½ in. (6 cm) wide on a piece of thin, corrugated cardboard and cut it out.

3 Staple the rectangle to one of the soles that you have cut out.

4 Glue the other two soles, one below and the other one on top of the first one, so that the staples will be concealed.

5 Paint green, red, and white stripes on the strip of cardboard.

To make the other flip-flop, follow the same steps. But be careful to copy the outline of the opposite foot! Now you're ready to flip-flop around!

Let your imagination soar

Other ideas:
You can make different designs for the straps on your flip-flops. You can also change the colors.

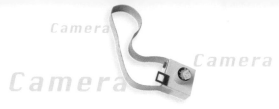

Camera

Become an expert photographer by making a camera out of a cardboard box. To do it, follow these steps carefully.

1 Cut off a piece about 1¼ in. (3 cm) long from the toilet tissue tube. This will be the lens.

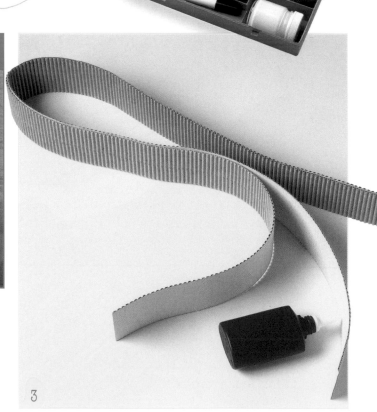

2 Draw a viewer on a piece of thin, smooth cardboard and cut it out.

3 Cut 2 strips of thin, corrugated cardboard to hang the camera from your neck and glue their smooth sides together.

50

4 Draw 5 small circles on a piece of heavy, smooth cardboard, cut them out and glue them all together. They will be the button of the camera.

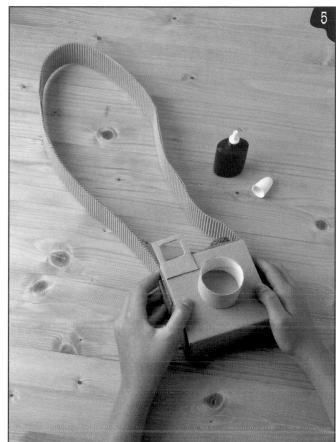

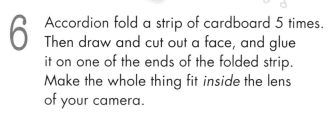

5 Glue all the accessories that you have made on the square box, as shown here.

6 Accordion fold a strip of cardboard 5 times. Then draw and cut out a face, and glue it on one of the ends of the folded strip. Make the whole thing fit *inside* the lens of your camera.

7 Glue the strip with the face inside the lens of the camera.

8 Use the flesh-colored paint to paint the face, the orange for the hair, black for the eyes and the nose, and red for the mouth.

9 Paint the rest of the camera with the colors of your choice.

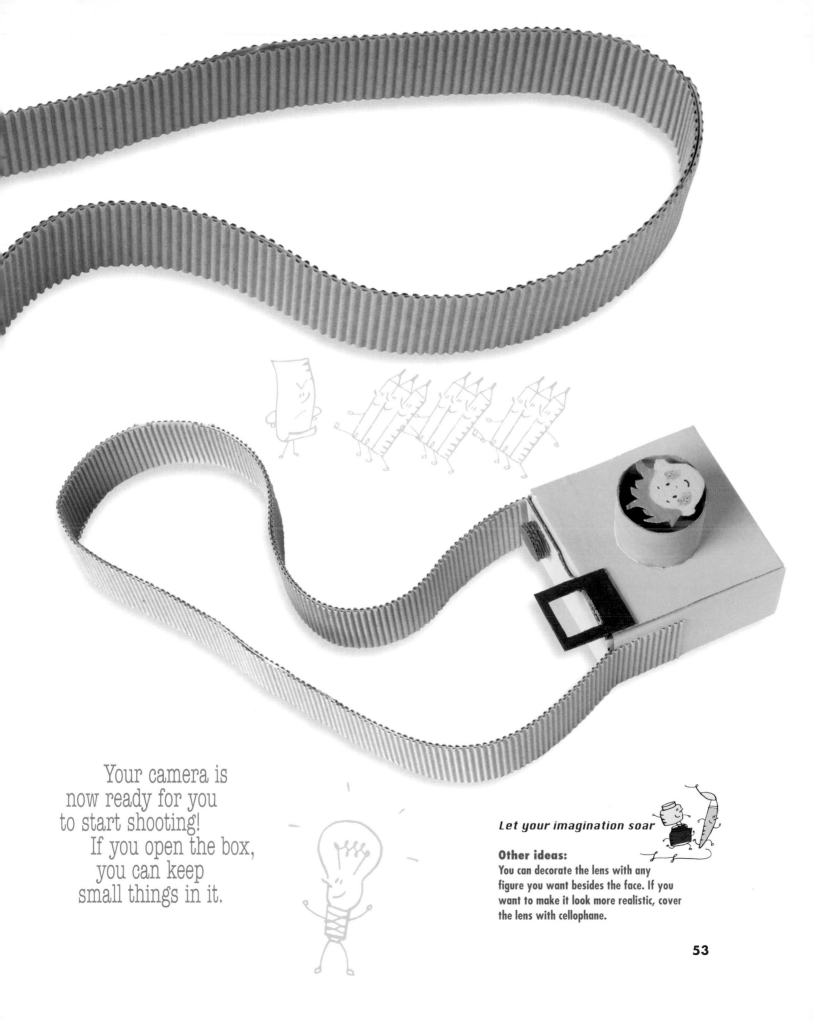

Your camera is
now ready for you
to start shooting!
If you open the box,
you can keep
small things in it.

Let your imagination soar

Other ideas:
You can decorate the lens with any
figure you want besides the face. If you
want to make it look more realistic, cover
the lens with cellophane.

53

Ring Toss Game

Would you like to make a friendly elephant to play with? If so, follow these steps carefully.

1 Draw a circle on a piece of thick, smooth cardboard using a large plate as a guide and cut it out.

2 Using a smaller plate as a guide, draw and cut out 2 ears on 2 other pieces of thick, smooth cardboard.

Toolbox

You will need:
- smooth, thick cardboard
- smooth, thin cardboard
- paper towel tube
- tape of different colors
- scissors
- glue
- pink, gray, red, orange, white, and blue paint
- paintbrush
- marker
- compass or different size plates (one small plate, one large)

3 Glue the 2 ears on the back side of the cut out circle and glue a cardboard tube in the center.

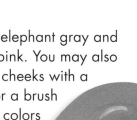

4 Paint the elephant gray and the ears pink. You may also paint the cheeks with a sponge or a brush using the colors of your choice.

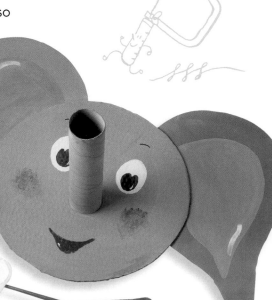

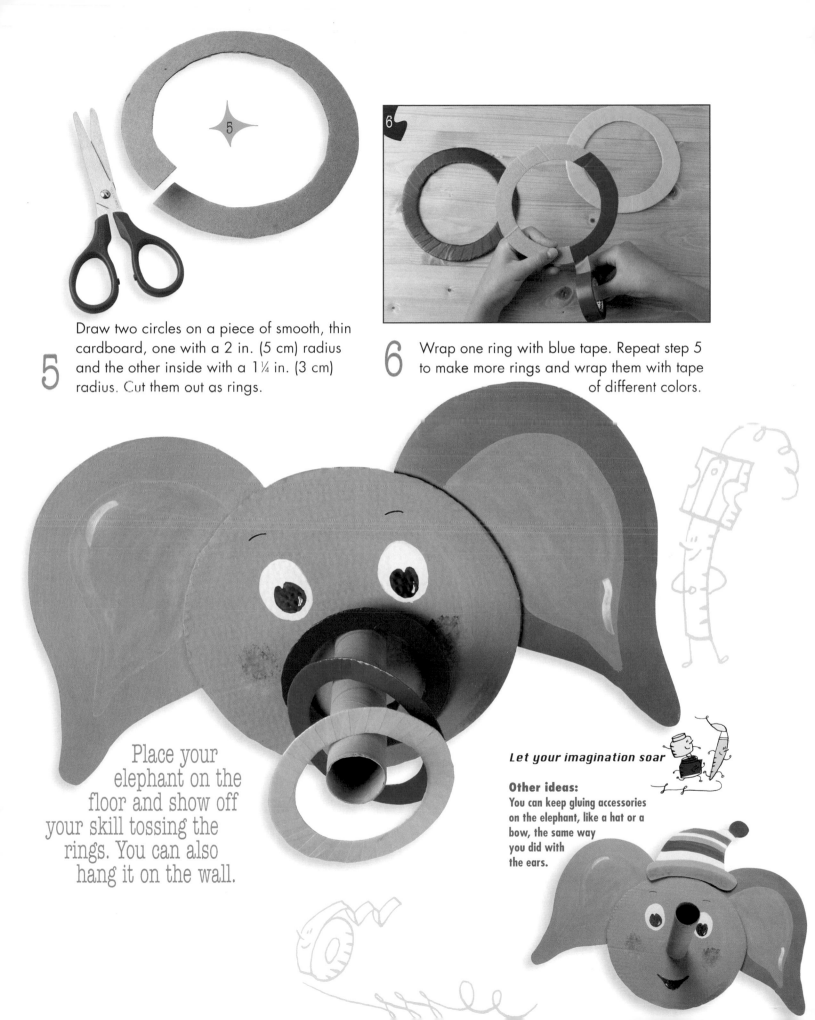

5 Draw two circles on a piece of smooth, thin cardboard, one with a 2 in. (5 cm) radius and the other inside with a 1¼ in. (3 cm) radius. Cut them out as rings.

6 Wrap one ring with blue tape. Repeat step 5 to make more rings and wrap them with tape of different colors.

Place your elephant on the floor and show off your skill tossing the rings. You can also hang it on the wall.

Let your imagination soar

Other ideas:
You can keep gluing accessories on the elephant, like a hat or a bow, the same way you did with the ears.

Pencil Holder

You can make an original pencil holder with cardboard tubes.
To do so you simply have to follow the step-by-step instructions.

1 Make a slit from top to bottom on each of the 3 toilet tissue tubes.

2 Attach the tubes with staples to make a clover shape.

3 Glue the tubes to a piece of cardboard 4½ × 4½ in. (12 × 12 cm). This will be the base of the pencil holder.

4 When the glue dries, cut the base into a rounded shape with scissors.

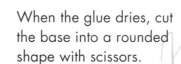

Toolbox

You will need:
- smooth, thick cardboard
- 3 toilet tissue tubes
- scissors
- glue
- stapler
- paint of different colors
- paintbrush
- marker

5 Paint the pencil holder with your favorite colors inside and out.

Gather all your color pencils and keep them in this holder that you have created.

Let your imagination soar

Other ideas:
You can combine more tubes and make other shapes. You can also decorate your holder with different designs of your choice and change the colors.

Coin Bank Doll

Where can you put your savings? With little more than a cardboard tube, you can rest assured that your savings will be protected. Follow these steps.

1 Near the top of a cardboard tube (about ⅓ of the way from the top) draw and cut a rectangular slot that will be easy to fit coins through.

2 Color the tube with blue paint and when it is dry, decorate it with white flowers.

Toolbox

You will need:
- thin, corrugated cardboard
- smooth, thick cardboard
- smooth, light cardboard
- 2 paper towel tubes
- scissors
- glue
- white, blue, red, green, and yellow paint
- paintbrush
- marker

3 Draw and cut out the shape of a face on a piece of smooth, thin cardboard. Also draw and cut out feet (from a piece of thick cardboard).

5 Cut a piece about 1¼ in. (3 cm) wide from the other tube to make the lid of the coin bank. Roll a strip of thin, corrugated cardboard so that it will fit into the tube you have just cut out, and glue it to the inside.

4 Color the feet and the face of the doll with paints of different colors.

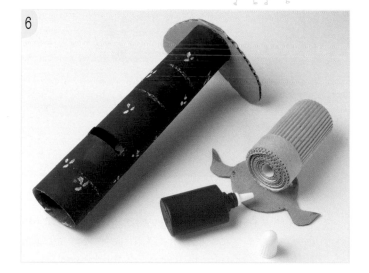

6 Glue the feet of the doll to the base of the painted tube and the face to the lid of the coin bank.

Let your imaginations soar

Other ideas:
You can change the face and turn your bank into an animal, like a cat.

Now all you have to do is put the lid on the coin bank. This doll can help you save a lot of money.

Drawers

Where do you keep your things? You can make yourself some drawers by following these steps.

Toolbox

You will need:
- smooth, light cardboard
- 2 boxes
- scissors
- glue
- green, orange, and blue paint
- paintbrush
- marker
- ruler

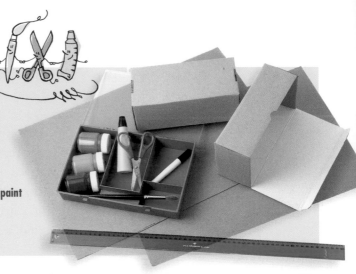

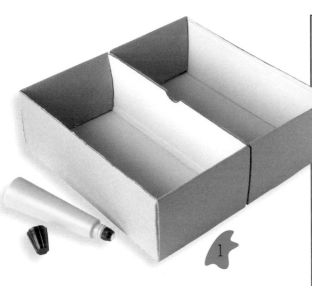

1 Glue two boxes of the same size side by side.

2 With the help of an adult, draw 3 open boxes on a piece of cardboard. One of them should be slightly smaller than one of the boxes. The other 2 should be half as large. Remember to make tabs for assembling the boxes.

3 After you cut them out, fold them along the lines and glue them together.

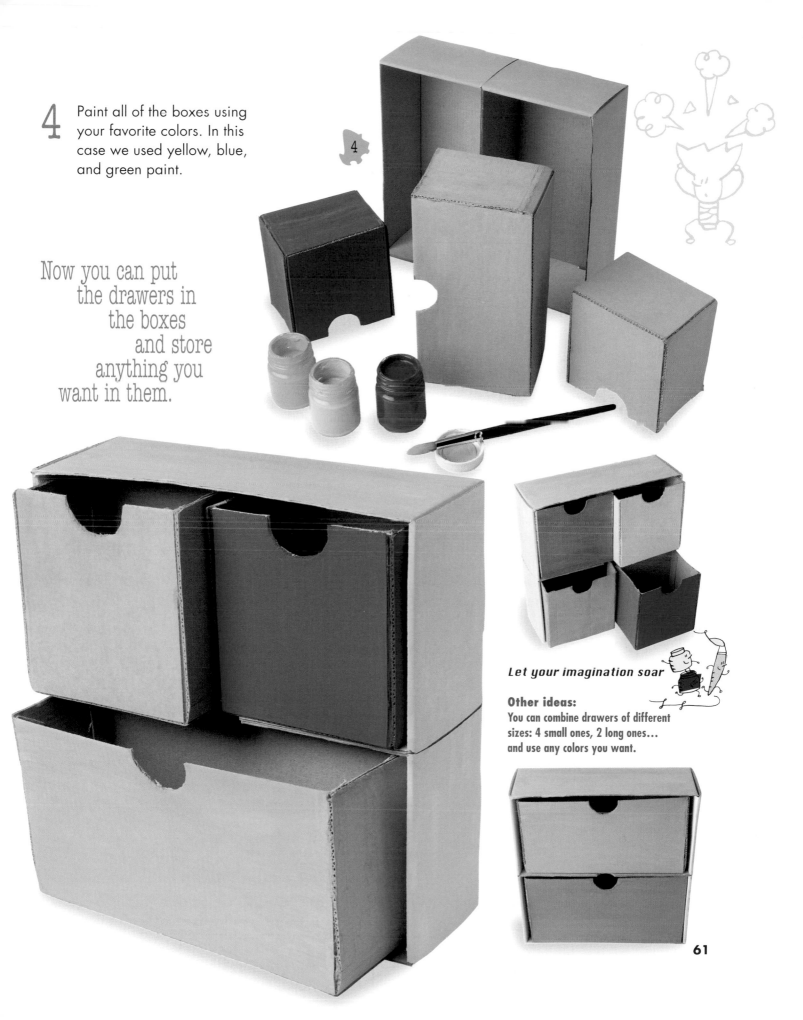

4 Paint all of the boxes using your favorite colors. In this case we used yellow, blue, and green paint.

Now you can put the drawers in the boxes and store anything you want in them.

Let your imagination soar

Other ideas:
You can combine drawers of different sizes: 4 small ones, 2 long ones... and use any colors you want.

61

Balancing Parrot

Do you think you can make a parrot that can hang onto a shelf and even dance on it?
In order for your parrot to become an acrobat follow these steps carefully.

Toolbox

You will need:
- smooth, light cardboard
- scissors
- glue
- green and other colored paints
- paintbrush
- marker
- modeling clay

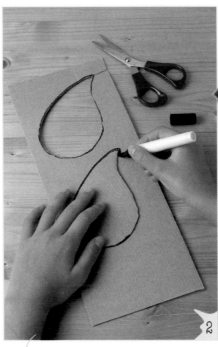

1 Draw the body of the parrot on a piece of smooth, light cardboard and cut it out.

2 Draw and cut out two wings from a different piece of the same cardboard.

3 Glue the wings to the body of the parrot, one on each side.

4 Paint the parrot green, placing it on a piece of cardboard to prevent the table from getting dirty.

5 Paint the feathers, the beak, and the eyes of the parrot with different colors.

Have you been able to balance your parrot? If not, add or take away modeling clay until you can do it.

6 Attach enough modeling clay to the tail of the parrot to keep it balanced on a shelf when hanging by its beak.

Let your imagination soar

Other ideas:
You can make other balancing animals or figures, for example, a monkey, a clown...

Case for Scissors

**Make a case and put your scissors in it so they do not hurt anybody by accident.
You can make it by following these simple steps.**

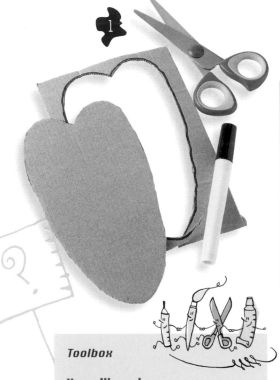

Toolbox

You will need:
- light, smooth cardboard
- light, corrugated cardboard
- scissors
- stapler
- pink, red, white, green, and black paint
- paintbrush
- marker

1 Draw the outline of a pair of scissors on a piece of light, smooth cardboard, leaving a margin of approximately ⅜ in. (1 cm). Then cut it out.

2 Use the piece you just cut out to trace the pocket for your case. Keep in mind that the pocket should be shorter so the scissors stick out.

3 Paint pink stripes on the pocket piece of light corrugated cardboard.

4

4 Staple both pieces of cardboard together and paint a pair of eyes and a nose on the back piece.

When the paint is dry, you can put the scissors inside the case.

Let your imagination soar

Other ideas:
You can make a larger case to keep other things in. You can also change the colors.

Picture Frame

Would you like to frame your favorite picture? You can make your own frame. Simply follow these steps.

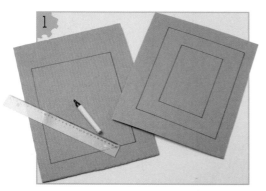

1 Draw an 8 × 10 in. (20 × 25 cm) rectangle on a piece of smooth, heavy cardboard. Do the same on a smooth, light piece and draw a rectangle inside it a little smaller than the picture you want to frame.

2 Cut out the rectangles, including the one you have drawn inside, to turn it into a frame.

3 Glue the frame to the smooth, heavy cardboard rectangle, leaving one of its sides open.

4 Cut 2 – 8 in. (20 cm) strips of thin, corrugated cardboard and 2 more 19½ in. (50 cm) long.

5 Glue the strips of thin, corrugated cardboard around the frame. Form wavy shapes on the 2 longer sides holding them in place with clothespins until the glue dries.

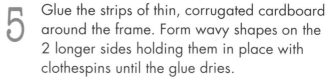

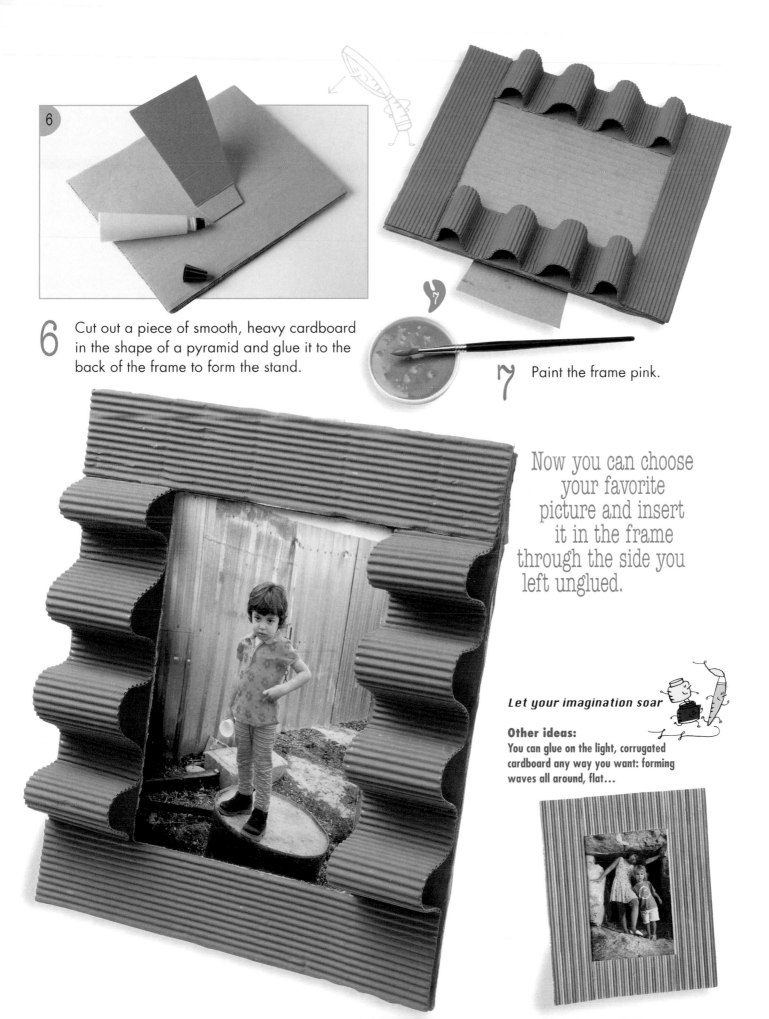

6 Cut out a piece of smooth, heavy cardboard in the shape of a pyramid and glue it to the back of the frame to form the stand.

7 Paint the frame pink.

Now you can choose your favorite picture and insert it in the frame through the side you left unglued.

Let your imagination soar

Other ideas:
You can glue on the light, corrugated cardboard any way you want: forming waves all around, flat...

Let's Create!

Fabrics

Bird

Let's create a beautiful bird from a simple sponge cloth.
Follow these steps carefully.

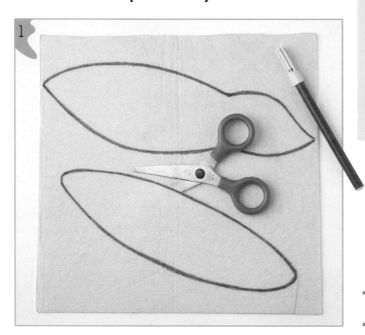

1 With a red marker draw the outlines of the body and the wings on a yellow sponge cloth, and cut them out.

2 Make a slit in the bird's body, which will later be used to insert the wing.

3 Draw and cut out the tail, the beak, and the eyes of the bird on a green sponge cloth. Remember to make two of each piece.

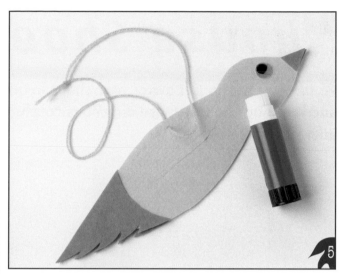

4 Glue the tail, the beak, and the eyes to each side of the bird's body.

5 Cut out the pupils from the black felt and glue them on the eyes. Make a little hole on the back of the bird and put a piece of yellow string through it for hanging.

Insert the wing in the slit that you made before and the bird is completed. As you can see, the sponge cloth has been transformed into a happy bird.

Let your imagination soar

Other ideas:
By practically following the same steps you can make an airplane...

71

House Shoe-Bag

House Shoe-Bag

House Shoe-Bag

House Shoe-Bag

Would you like to put away your shoes in an original and fun way? Follow these directions carefully to make your house shoe-bag.

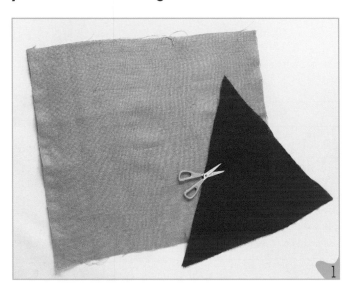

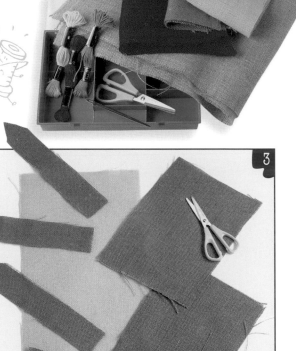

1 To make the roof, cut out a piece of red sackcloth in the shape of a triangle. Then for the front of the house, cut out a rectangle from a piece of brown fabric. The short sides should measure the same as the base of the roof.

2 Attach the roof and the front of the house with red thread and a large-eyed needle.

3 Cut out 2 rectangles from a piece of green sackcloth for the windows. Then cut a rectangle from a piece of yellow fabric that is as long as the base of the front of the house and as wide as the length of your shoes. Finally, cut out 4 strips of green fabric to make a fence.

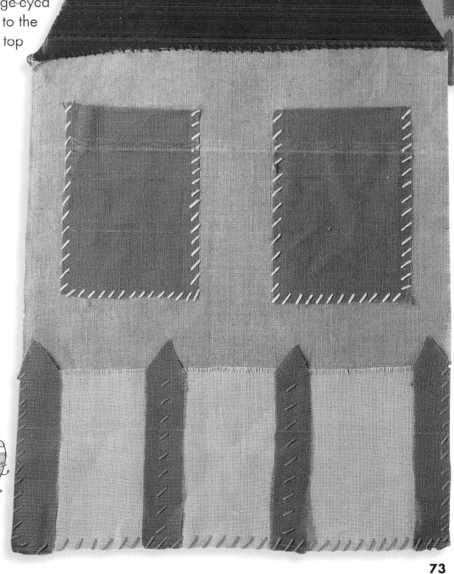

4 Using yellow thread and a large-eyed needle, attach the 2 windows to the front of the house, leaving the top part unsewed.

5 Sew the yellow rectangle to the front of the house along the bottom. Finally, sew on the 4 green strips, the 2 middle ones on each side of the center to separate the 3 pockets.

Let your imagination soar

Other ideas:
You can invent any shape for the shoe-bag: a train, a kangaroo, a tree...

Braided Doll

You can give life to a skein of yarn by creating a beautiful braided doll! To do it, follow these directions.

1 With the help of a friend make an oval ring with green yarn and tie it on one of the sides with colored yarn. Then cut the ring on the opposite side.

Toolbox

You will need:
- scissors
- white glue
- black felt
- one skein of green yarn and another of mixed colors

2 Following the same procedure make another ring, but this one should be smaller and made with different colored yarns, which will be the hair. Put the two bunches together.

3 Next, using colored yarn, tie a knot at approximately 2 inches (5 cm) below the hair. Now you have the doll's head.

4 To make the arms, separate 2 bunches of yarn and tie another knot with green yarn at the height that would be the waist. Make the legs by separating the remaining yarn into 2 more bunches.

5 Braid the arms and the legs and tie them at the ends.

6 Cut out 2 eyes from black felt and glue them onto the face of the doll. Finally, arrange the hair as you wish.

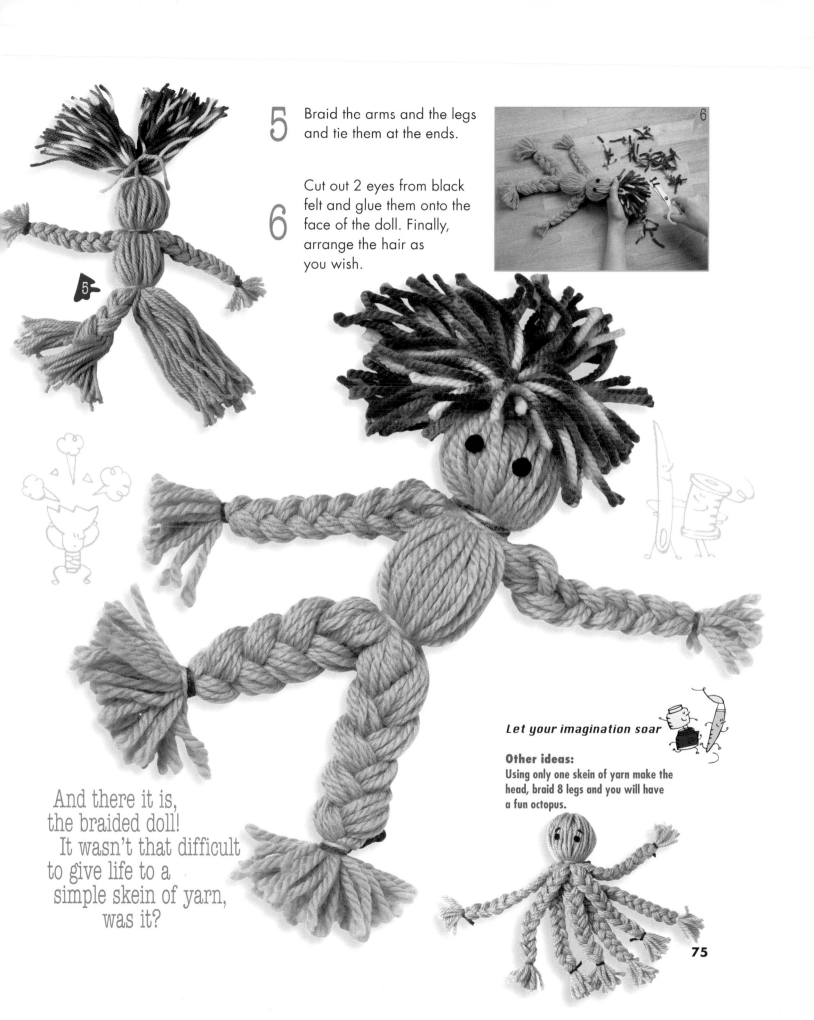

And there it is, the braided doll! It wasn't that difficult to give life to a simple skein of yarn, was it?

Let your imagination soar

Other ideas:
Using only one skein of yarn make the head, braid 8 legs and you will have a fun octopus.

75

Ball

With only a few socks and polyester fiberfill you can make a great ball. To design it follow these directions.

Toolbox

You will need:
- scissors
- orange, white, red, and blue stockings
- polyester fiberfill

1 Cut off part of a red stocking below the knee.

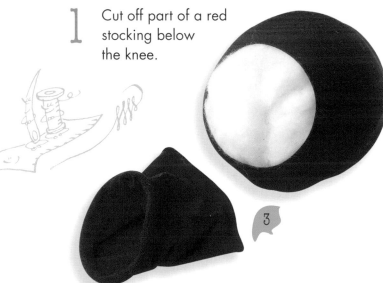

2 Insert the fiberfill material through the opening until a very firm ball has been formed.

3 Cut off the leftover piece of stocking to make a round ball.

4 Pinch different parts of the white, blue, and orange stockings and cut them to make holes.

76

5 Insert the ball into the white stocking and cut off the excess part of the stocking.

6 Follow the same procedure as in step 5 with the blue and orange stockings.

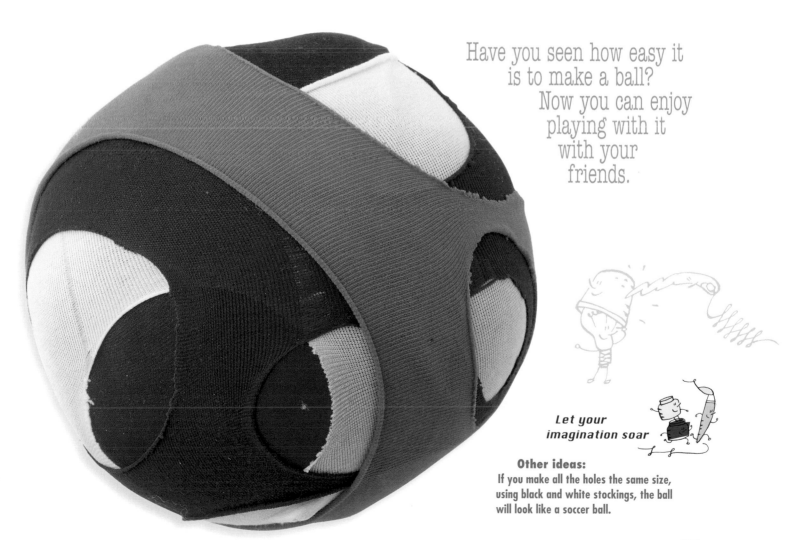

Have you seen how easy it is to make a ball? Now you can enjoy playing with it with your friends.

Let your imagination soar

Other ideas:
If you make all the holes the same size, using black and white stockings, the ball will look like a soccer ball.

Car with Trailer

With this entertaining craft project you will be able to add a new car model to your collection. To design it follow these steps.

1 Make a pattern of the car by drawing the outline on a piece of poster board and then cutting it out.

Toolbox

You will need:
- scissors
- large-eyed needle
- red marker
- white glue
- green sponge cloth
- orange sponge cloth
- maroon yarn
- black felt
- orange felt
- 2 sheets of orange poster board

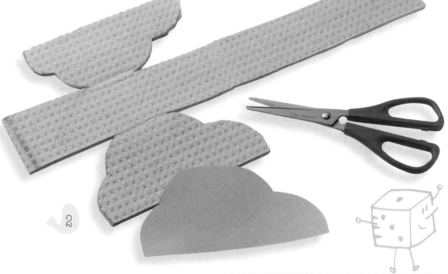

2 Using the pattern as a guide, trace two outlines of the car on a green sponge cloth attached to a strip 14 in. (35 cm) long and 2.3 in. (6 cm) wide. Cut out the shape in one piece.

3 Using a large-eyed needle sew the piece with maroon yarn.

4 Draw 5 windows, 4 for the sides and one for the front, on a piece of black felt, and 2 headlights on a piece of orange felt, and cut them all out.

5 Glue all these pieces to their respective places on the car.

6 To make the wheels, cut out 4 strips of orange felt 10 in. (25 cm) long by ⅝ in. (1.5 cm) wide, and 4 strips of black felt 8 in. (20 cm) long by ⅝ in. (1.5 cm) wide. Place the black felt on top of the orange one and roll them together. Glue the end with white glue.

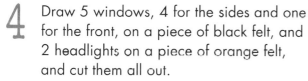

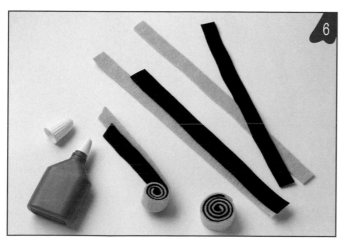

7 Glue the 4 wheels onto the car with white glue.

8 Draw the pattern of the trailer on poster board. The base should be approximately 3 in. (8 cm) long by 2 in. (5 cm) wide, and the sides 1½ in. (4 cm) high. Cut out the shape.

9 Trace the pattern of the trailer on a piece of green sponge cloth and cut it out.

10 Cut out a strip of orange felt 10 in. (26 cm) long by ⅜ in. (.96 cm) wide and use it to hold the 4 sides of the trailer together by gluing it with white glue.

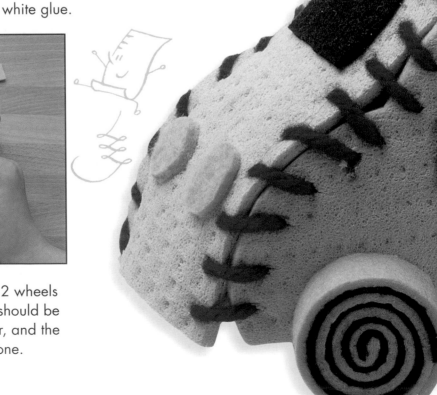

11 Following step number 7, make the 2 wheels for the trailer. In this case the strips should be shorter so the wheels can be smaller, and the orange strip will go over the black one.

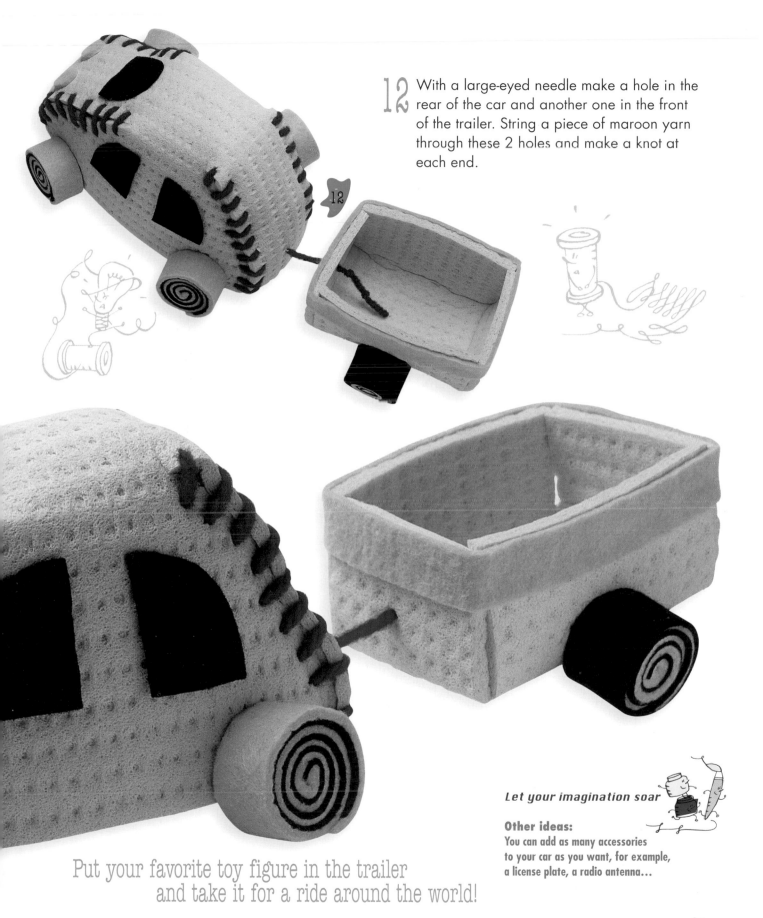

12 With a large-eyed needle make a hole in the rear of the car and another one in the front of the trailer. String a piece of maroon yarn through these 2 holes and make a knot at each end.

Put your favorite toy figure in the trailer and take it for a ride around the world!

Let your imagination soar

Other ideas:
You can add as many accessories to your car as you want, for example, a license plate, a radio antenna...

Sock Puppet

Make a sock come to life by turning it into a playful puppet.
Follow these steps to make your puppet.

1 Make a cut near the toe of the sock. This cut should be approximately 1 in. (3 cm).

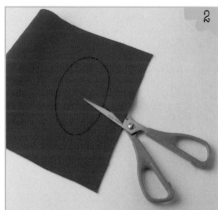

2 Cut out an oval from a piece of red felt about 3 in. (8 cm) long.

3 Turn the sock inside out and sew the red oval over the opening that you have previously made. Now you have the puppet's mouth.

4 Cut out eyes from a piece of black felt and glue them onto 2 orange pom-poms (or any other color you want).

Have your friends create a sock puppet of their own and entertain people with your wonderful characters!

5 Finally, attach the pom-poms with double-sided tape above the mouth of the puppet, opposite the heel.

Let your imagination soar

Other ideas:
You can give your puppet wonderful hairstyles with different pom-poms.

Organizer

With this fun and easy craft project you can make a beautiful organizer for your pencils. To design it, follow these steps carefully.

Toolbox

You will need:
- scissors
- stapler
- piece of string 27 in. (70 cm) long
- yellow sponge cloth 16 × 16 in. (40 × 40 cm)
- green sponge cloth
- ruler
- black marker

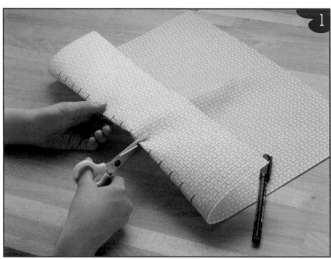

1 4 in. (10 cm) from one of the edges of the yellow sponge cloth, make 16 – ⅝ in. (1.5 cm) cuts. Leave a ¾ in. (2 cm) space between the cuts.

2 Cut a strip of green sponge cloth ⅝ in. (1.5 cm) wide by 18 in. (45 cm) long.

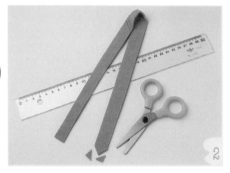

3 Weave the green strip through the cuts that you made before.

4 Staple the strip at the two edges of the sponge cloth.

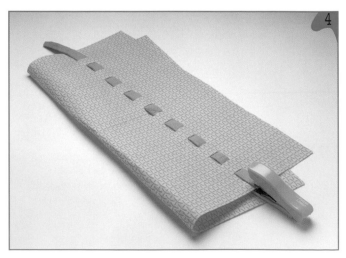

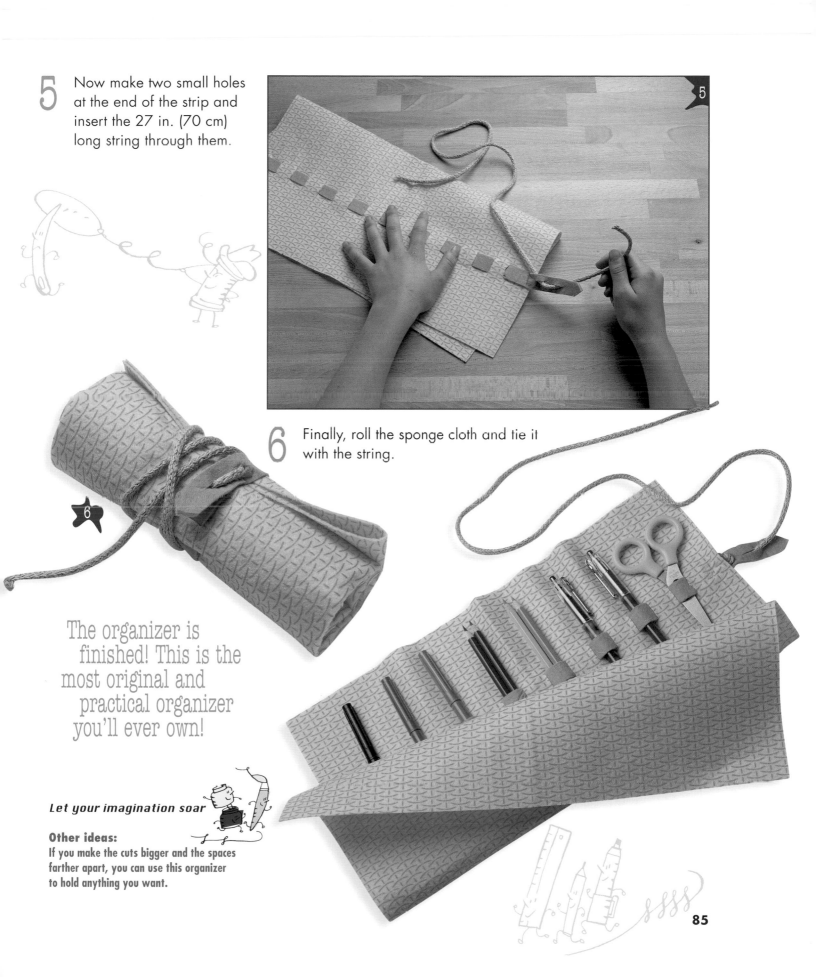

5 Now make two small holes at the end of the strip and insert the 27 in. (70 cm) long string through them.

6 Finally, roll the sponge cloth and tie it with the string.

The organizer is finished! This is the most original and practical organizer you'll ever own!

Let your imagination soar

Other ideas:
If you make the cuts bigger and the spaces farther apart, you can use this organizer to hold anything you want.

Yarn Bug

You can create a little best friend to take with you wherever you go. To make it, follow these steps carefully.

Toolbox

You will need:
- scissors
- cardboard
- white glue
- two-tone blue yarn
- black marker
- flesh-colored felt
- black felt
- white felt

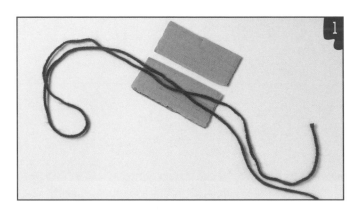

1 Cut out two pieces of cardboard 2 in. (5 cm) wide and 3 in. (8 cm) long. Then cut a piece of blue yarn 16 in. (40 cm) long and put it, folded in half, between the two pieces.

2 Wrap some two-tone blue yarn around the cardboard pieces. Note that the more yarn you wrap around, the puffier your ball will be.

3 Tie a knot with the two ends of the 16 in. (40 cm) piece of yarn that hangs from either end of the cardboard.

4 Separate the cardboard pieces from the yarn and cut it all the way around to make the ball.

86

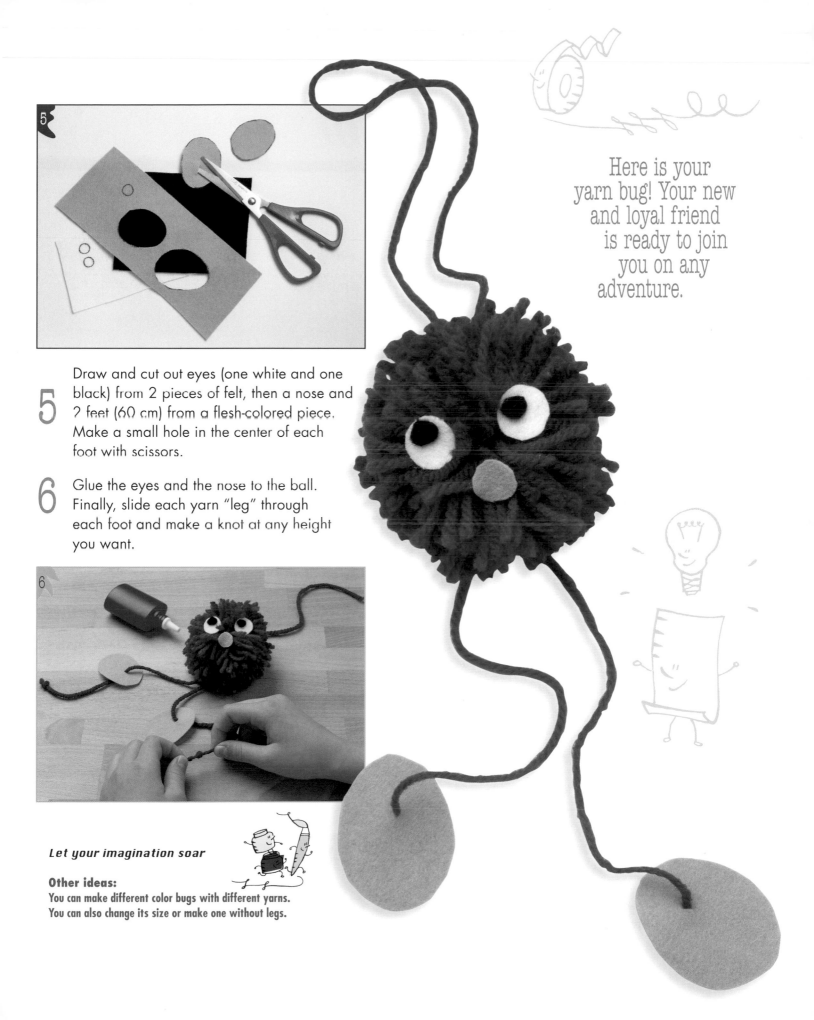

Here is your yarn bug! Your new and loyal friend is ready to join you on any adventure.

5 Draw and cut out eyes (one white and one black) from 2 pieces of felt, then a nose and 2 feet (60 cm) from a flesh-colored piece. Make a small hole in the center of each foot with scissors.

6 Glue the eyes and the nose to the ball. Finally, slide each yarn "leg" through each foot and make a knot at any height you want.

Let your imagination soar

Other ideas:
You can make different color bugs with different yarns. You can also change its size or make one without legs.

Pajama Pillow

If you want to put away your pajamas neatly and to be more comfortable than ever at the same time, design this original pajama storage pillow. To make it, follow these steps carefully.

Toolbox

You will need:
- scissors
- green and yellow cotton thread
- large-eyed needle
- heavy fabric (red and yellow)
- polyester fiberfill

1 With a large-eyed needle and yellow cotton-blend thread sew 2 pieces of red cloth, on three sides only.

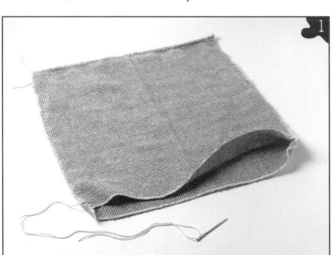

2 Insert the filling through the side that you have not sewed.

3 Close the pillow by sewing the open side with green cotton-blend thread.

4 To make the pocket, fold the yellow cloth in half and sew it with green cotton-blend thread.

There it is, the pajama pillow! Do you know a more "comfortable" way of storing your pajamas?

Let your imagination soar

Other ideas:
You can make the pillow with different colors or make a flap to close the pocket.

Bookmark

If you always want to remember the page where you left off reading, put together this bookmark. To make it, follow these directions step-by-step.

1 Cut out a strip of tan poster board 10 in. (25 cm) long by 3 in. (8 cm) wide.

2 Draw a T-shirt on the cotton-blend print fabric and pants on the denim fabric and then cut them out.

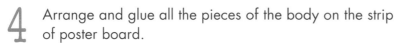

3 Cut out the hair and shoes from a piece of black felt, and a face from a piece of flesh-colored felt.

4 Arrange and glue all the pieces of the body on the strip of poster board.

5 Cut out the shape of the body and form the hands with scissors.

Now you have the finished project. Your bookmark person will reach up to hold your place!

Let your imagination soar

Other ideas:
You can make the figure in various poses and dress it with fabrics of different prints.

Caterpillar

Would you like to have a new friend? Then have fun creating this fluffy and friendly caterpillar. To make it, follow these steps carefully.

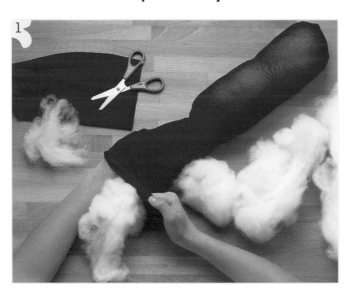

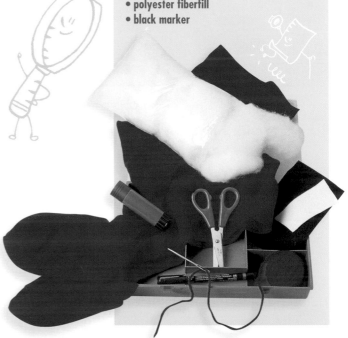

1 Cut off the stocking at the knee and insert the fiberfill material. Make a knot at the end.

2 Make the rings of the caterpillar by tying it with red yarn. You will have to make 6 in all, 5 big ones and a smaller one for the nose.

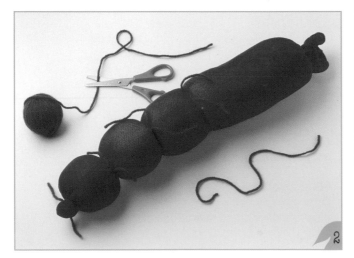

3 Cut out the eyes for the caterpillar from pieces of black and white felt. Then cut out 4 circles from black felt to make the spots.

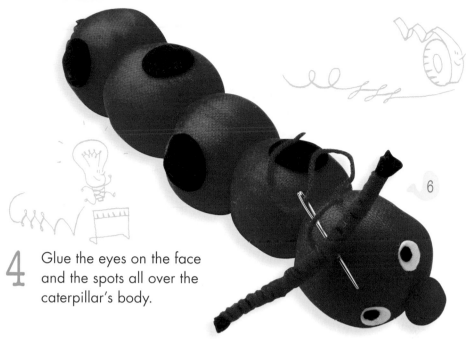

4 Glue the eyes on the face and the spots all over the caterpillar's body.

5 Roll a piece of black felt and tie it with red yarn to make the antennae.

6 Then sew the antennae to the head of the caterpillar with a large-eyed needle.

You have finished the caterpillar!
Isn't it easy to make new friends?

Let your imagination soar

Other ideas:
You can make different rings by using stockings of assorted colors or you can decorate the body of the caterpillar with other shapes.

Bag

With just a pair of scissors, felt, and yarn, you can put together a useful and colorful bag. To make it, follow the instructions step-by-step.

Toolbox

You will need:
- scissors
- black marker
- blue felt
- yellow felt
- black yarn
- ruler
- needle

1 Cut out 2 strips of felt, one blue and one yellow, 10 in. (25 cm) wide. The blue one should be 28 in. (70 cm) long and the yellow one only 16 in. (40 cm).

2 Make a small mark every ¾ in. (2 cm) on both edges of the blue piece with a black marker. Repeat this procedure on the yellow piece.

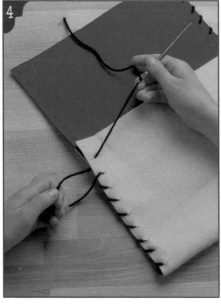

3 Make a small hole on each mark with the point of the scissors. To make this task easier, pinch together the border of the pieces of felt with your fingers.

4 Fold the piece of blue felt in half and the yellow one over it, and sew the edges with black yarn.

5 Cut out 9 lengths of yarn. Tie a knot at one end and make a braid.

6 Tic the braid to the two holes at the top of the bag.

Now you have a beautiful bag with three pockets to carry anything you want!

Let your imagination soar

Other ideas:
You can decorate the bag with different designs or glue new pockets on it.

Clay

Monkey

Imagine a monkey hanging on a vine from the ceiling of your bedroom! You can create one with modeling clay by carefully following these steps.

Toolbox

You will need:
- brown, white, black, yellow, orange, and flesh-colored modeling clay.
- strainer
- awl or large needle
- plastic knife
- rolling pin
- cord

1   Make a coil with brown modeling clay and form two ears on one of the ends.

2   Make a flesh-colored ball and attach it to the face by pressing it with your fingers. Make the nostrils and mouth with a large needle.

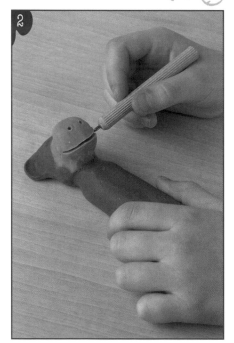

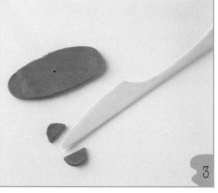

3   Flatten a piece of flesh-colored clay with a rolling pin and cut out the belly and two ears with the knife. Mark the belly button with the needle.

4   To make the eyes, form two white balls and two smaller black ones and attach them to the face.

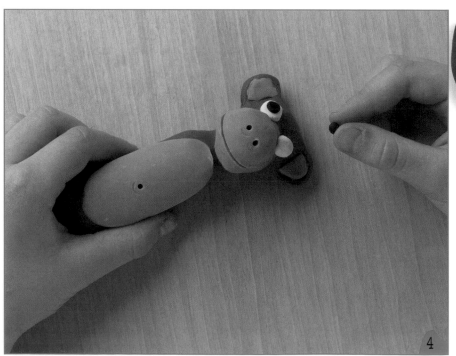

98

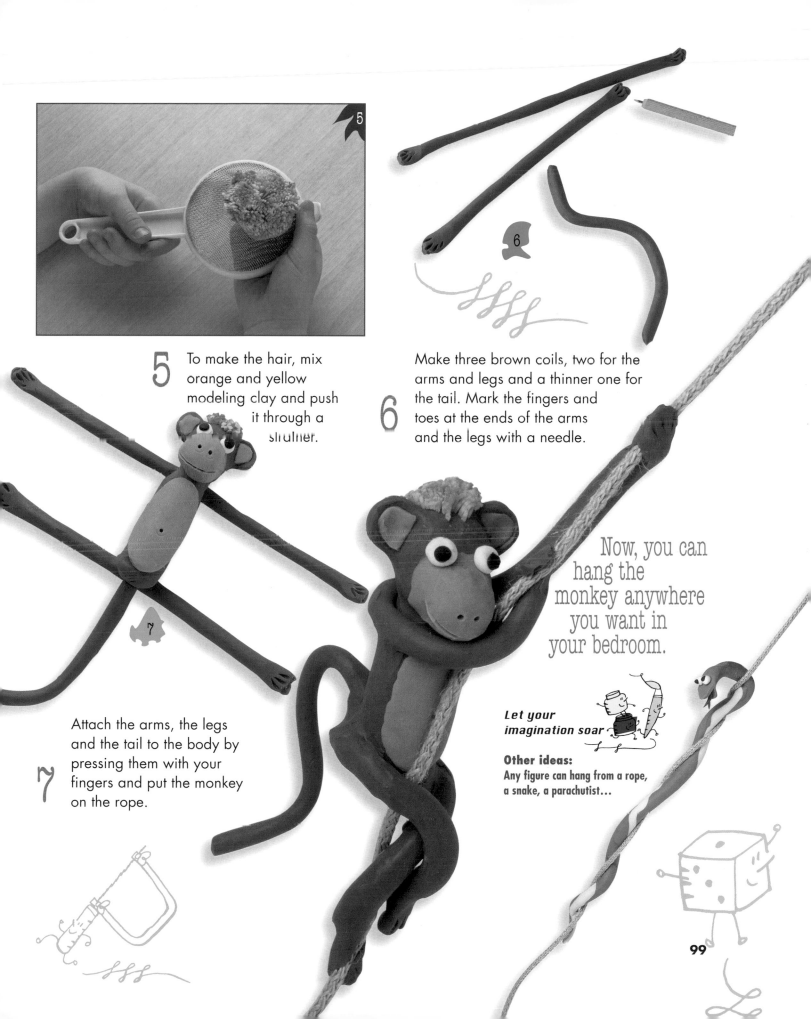

5 To make the hair, mix orange and yellow modeling clay and push it through a strainer.

6 Make three brown coils, two for the arms and legs and a thinner one for the tail. Mark the fingers and toes at the ends of the arms and the legs with a needle.

7 Attach the arms, the legs and the tail to the body by pressing them with your fingers and put the monkey on the rope.

Now, you can hang the monkey anywhere you want in your bedroom.

Let your imagination soar

Other ideas:
Any figure can hang from a rope, a snake, a parachutist...

Magnet
Magnet
Magnet

Magnet

If you want to decorate the refrigerator with fun magnets, make them yourself. Simply follow the step-by-step instructions.

1 Flatten a piece of blue modeling clay with the help of a rolling pin and draw a fish on it.

2 Cut out the outline of the fish with a plastic knife and decorate it with dots using a needle.

Toolbox

You will need:
- blue, white, black, green, red, and orange modeling clay
- rolling pin
- awl or large needle
- magnet
- plastic knife
- latex varnish
- paintbrush
- glue

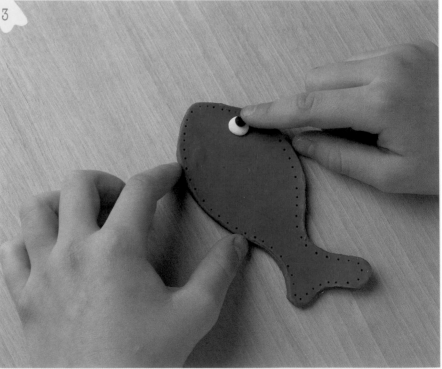

3 Make a small white ball and another smaller black one and attach them to the face of the fish by pressing them with your finger.

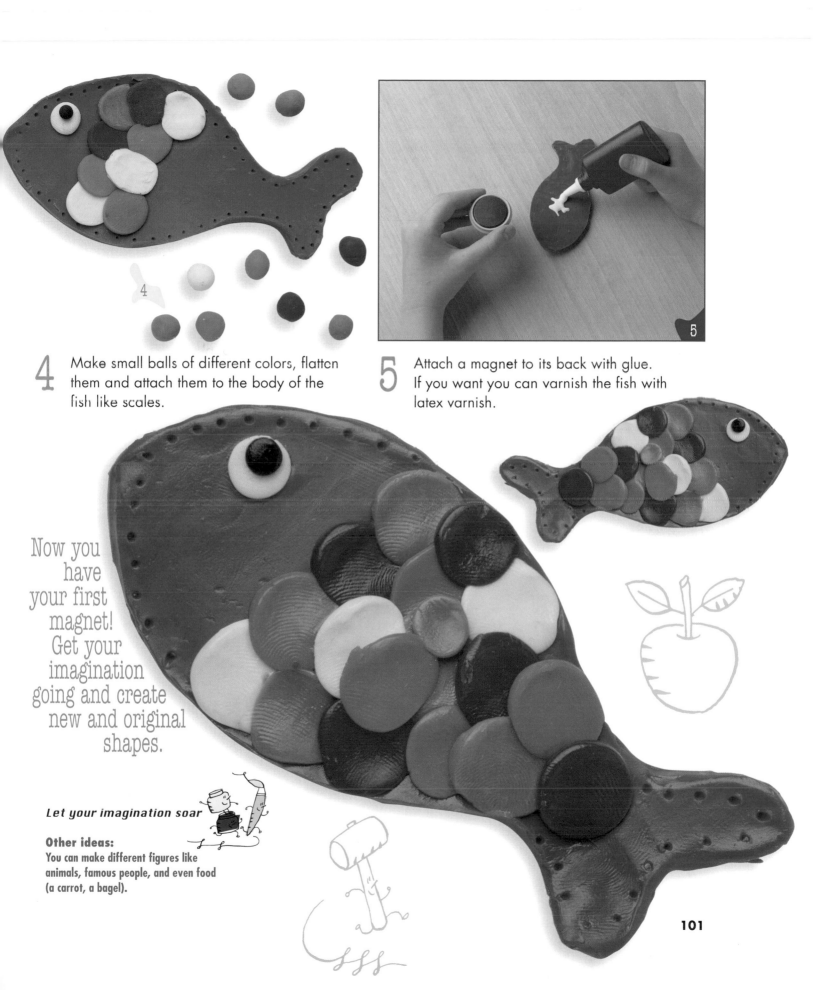

4 Make small balls of different colors, flatten them and attach them to the body of the fish like scales.

5 Attach a magnet to its back with glue. If you want you can varnish the fish with latex varnish.

Now you have your first magnet! Get your imagination going and create new and original shapes.

Let your imagination soar

Other ideas:
You can make different figures like animals, famous people, and even food (a carrot, a bagel).

101

Coaster

Coaster

Coaster

Coaster

You can make decorative coasters with modeling clay and a sheet of clear plastic. Simply follow the step-by-step instructions.

1 Make two coils with modeling clay, one white and one purple, and form a spiral. Place it on a piece of clear plastic.

2 Make an orange coil and wrap it around the spiral.

3 Make a red coil and wrap it around the orange.

4 Lay a piece of clear plastic over the modeling clay and flatten it with a rolling pin.

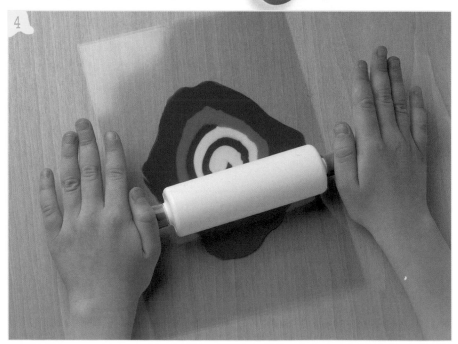

5 Cut out the plastic sheets with scissors following the shape of the rolled clay.

You can put your glass on it without worrying about staining the table!

Let your imagination soar

Other ideas:
You can create many designs by arranging the clay in different shapes, for example, a flower.

Let's Eat!

Would you like to cook pretend food with clay? Want to invite your friends for lunch? Follow these steps, and your guests will be licking their fingers.

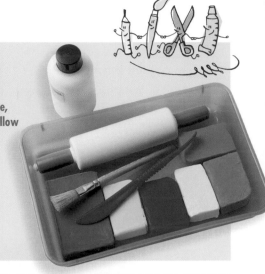

Toolbox

You will need:
- blue, white, orange, green, red, and yellow modeling clay
- plastic knife
- rolling pin
- latex varnish
- paintbrush

1 Flatten a piece of blue modeling clay with a rolling pin and cut out an oval shape. This will be the base of the plate.

2 Make a coil with modeling clay of the same color and attach it to the base by pressing the edges with your fingers.

3 Form little white balls, flatten them and attach them to the border of the plate.

4 Flatten a piece of white modeling clay and cut it into the shape of the white of a fried egg. To finish it up, make an orange ball and place it on top of the white for the yolk.

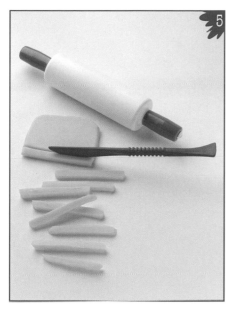

5

6

Flatten a piece of green modeling clay and cut out several uneven shapes, to make them look like lettuce. Also make a ball with red clay and cut it in four pieces for the tomato.

7

Put all the pieces on the plate and varnish them.

5 Flatten a piece of yellow modeling clay and cut it into long strips as if they were french fries.

Now decide who to invite. Lunch is served!

Let your imagination soar

Other ideas:
You can make spaghetti by pushing the clay through a strainer, or model all kinds of foods.

Doll

Doll
Doll
Doll

She wears big shoes, a bell-shaped dress and has green hair... You too can make a fun doll like this one. Simply follow these steps.

1 Form the feet and the legs with a piece of green modeling clay.

2 Flatten a piece of pink modeling clay with a rolling pin and cover the feet to make a pair of shoes.

Toolbox

You will need:
- pink, green, white, black, and flesh-colored modeling clay
- strainer
- toothpick
- rolling pin
- plastic knife

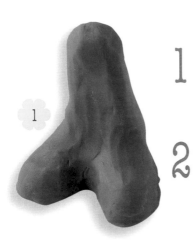

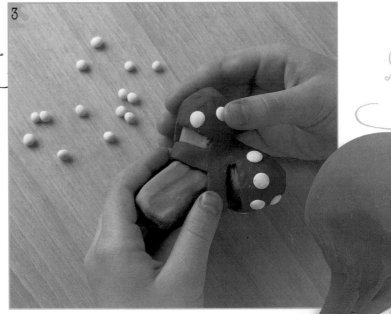

3 Then make little white balls and attach them to the shoes by pressing with your fingers.

4 Form a ball with the flesh-colored clay and insert a toothpick.

5 Form two little white balls and two smaller black ones for the eyes, two little pink balls for the cheeks, and a flesh-colored one for the nose.

To make the hair, form a ball with green modeling clay and press it through a strainer.

7 Flatten a piece of pink clay and cut out a half circle.

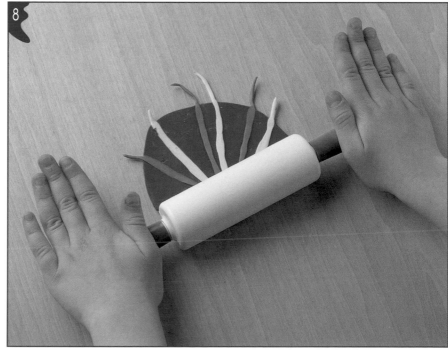

8 Form three very thin white coils and three green ones and place them on the pink clay. Then roll them with the rolling pin and cut off the overhanging ends.

9 To make the scarf, form three pink balls and three green. Make a white coil and flatten it with the rolling pin.

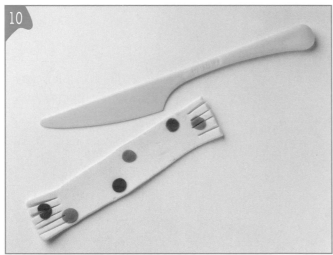

10 Attach the little balls to the scarf and flatten them with the rolling pin. Then make small cuts on each end to simulate the fringe.

11 Form a long pink coil to make the arms.

12 Insert the head with the toothpick into the legs.

108

13 Place the half circle with the stripes around the neck, forming a bell shape, and press it so it sticks to the toothpick.

14 Place the arms around the neck and then wrap the scarf around.

You have created a wonderful character! See how easy it was?

Let your imagination soar

Other ideas:
You can decorate the dress with polka dots and the scarf with stripes, and you can even give your figure long hair.

Martian Pencil Top

Would you like to turn your pencil into something unique? Just follow these steps.

1 Put a piece of green clay on the end of the pencil and model the head of the martian.

2 Make two little balls with orange modeling clay and place them on the ends of the antennae. Form the long nose and draw the mouth with an awl.

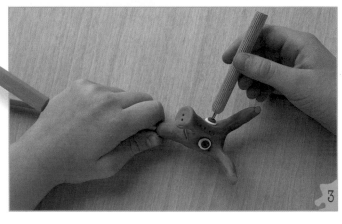

Toolbox

You will need:
- green, white, purple, and orange modeling clay
- pencil
- awl or large needle
- rolling pin
- plastic knife
- latex varnish
- paintbrush

3 To make the eyes, model two white balls and two smaller purple ones and attach them to the face by pressing with your fingers. Pierce holes in the eyes with an awl to make the pupils.

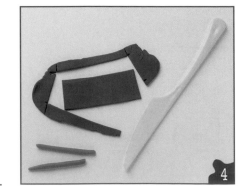

4 Flatten a piece of purple clay with a rolling pin and cut out a rectangle with the knife. Also make two coils, one orange and one green.

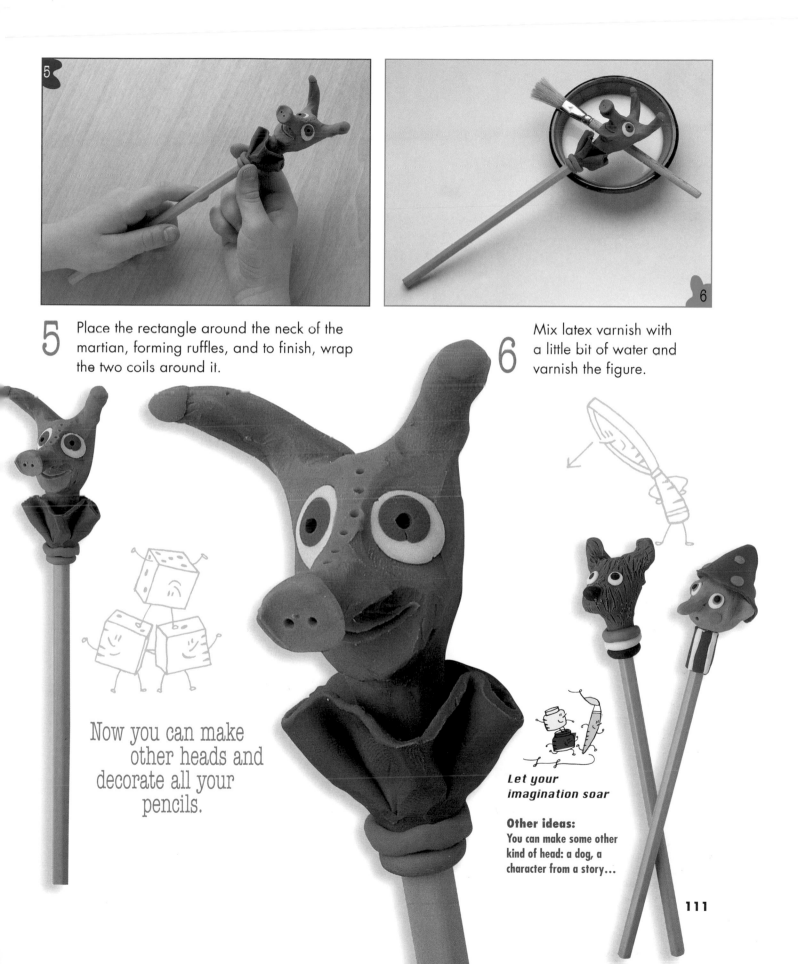

5 Place the rectangle around the neck of the martian, forming ruffles, and to finish, wrap the two coils around it.

6 Mix latex varnish with a little bit of water and varnish the figure.

Now you can make other heads and decorate all your pencils.

Let your imagination soar

Other ideas:
You can make some other kind of head: a dog, a character from a story...

Picture Clipboard

Make a picture that can also be used to hold your notes. Follow the process step-by-step.

Toolbox

You will need:
- light blue, dark blue, dark green, purple, white, orange, pink, and light green modeling clay
- rolling pin
- awl or large needle
- board 3 × 2¾ in. (16 × 14 cm) and ⅛ in. (3 mm) thick
- latex varnish
- paintbrush
- clothespin
- glue

1 Press and spread a piece of light blue modeling clay on the board to make the sky. Add a little bit of white clay to make the clouds.

2 Make two white coils and shape them into seagulls. Form the beaks with the orange clay.

3 Place the seagulls in the sky and make the sea covering the rest of the wood by mixing dark blue, purple, dark green, and white modeling clay.

4 Varnish the picture with latex varnish mixed with a little bit of water.

6 Make three little orange balls and place them on the boat. Use the awl to decorate the boat.

5 Roll out green and pink modeling clay with a rolling pin. Draw and cut out two boats with an awl or a plastic knife. Place the smaller green one over the pink boat.

7 Varnish the boat with latex varnish and glue it to the end of a clothespin. Then attach this to the sea with glue.

Notice how the clothespin for holding notes is also the mast of the ship.

Let your imagination soar

Other ideas:
You can attach two clothespins so you have two boats sailing or invent any other background (mountains, for example).

113

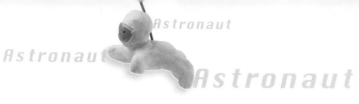
Astronaut

Create an astronaut-in-space mobile with modeling clay and wire. Simply follow these steps.

Toolbox

You will need:
- light blue, dark blue, white, purple, orange, red, yellow, and flesh-colored modeling clay
- rolling pin
- plastic knife
- awl or large needle
- blue-colored wire
- scissors

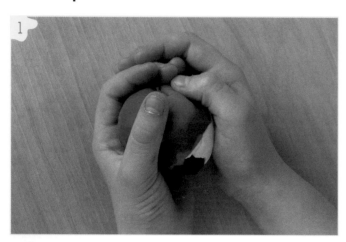

1 Form a ball mixing light blue, dark blue, white, purple, and orange modeling clay.

2 Make a ball smaller than the previous one mixing yellow and orange clay.

3 Form the body of an astronaut with white modeling clay. Use a little bit of flesh-colored clay for the face.

4 Make a coil with red modeling clay for the rocket. You can form the fins by flattening white clay, then attaching it to the body of the rocket.

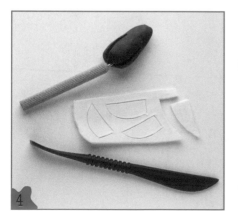

5 Cut a piece of blue wire about 5 in. (15 cm) long and twist one of the ends in a U shape.

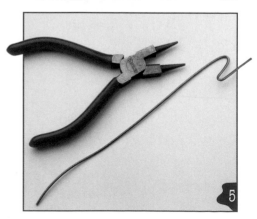

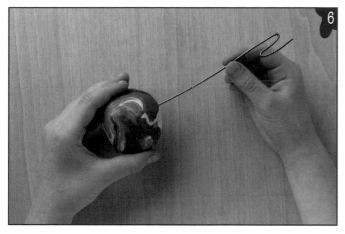

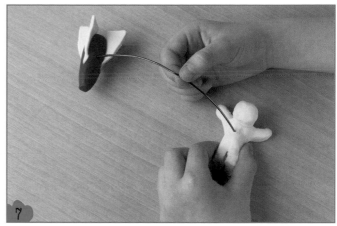

6 Insert the wire into the big ball (the Earth).

7 Cut another piece of blue wire about 8 in. (20 cm) long and attach the astronaut to one end and the rocket to the other.

8 Place the wire with the astronaut and the rocket on top of the other wire. Finish the mobile by pushing the small ball (the Moon) onto the end of the wire that is still empty.

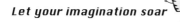

Let your imagination soar

Other ideas:
Instead of the rocket you can make a star or add other planets.

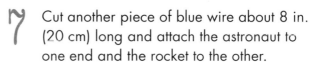

Your astronaut will now float in space.

Clothes Hanger Decoration

Toolbox

You will need:
- orange, red, purple, white, green, and black modeling clay
- rolling pin
- latex varnish
- paintbrush
- plastic knife
- awl or large needle
- glue
- green clothes hanger

Bring your clothes hangers to life by creating fun figures with modeling clay. Carefully follow these steps that tell how.

1 Make a coil with orange modeling clay and flatten it with the rolling pin.

2 Form very fine coils with red modeling clay and lay them across the orange strip. Then roll the pin over them.

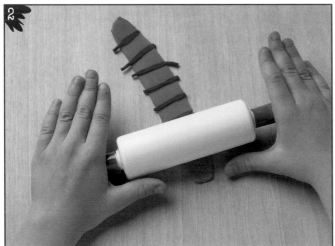

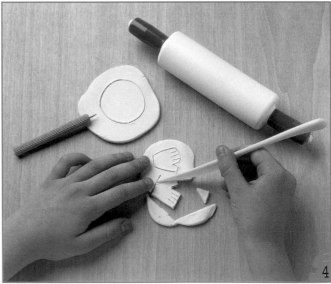

3 Cut the strip in two equal pieces and place one over the other at an angle.

4 Flatten a piece of white modeling clay and draw a circle (the face) and the two hands with the awl. Then cut out the parts with the knife and place the hands at the ends of the arms.

5 Flatten a piece of purple modeling clay and draw and cut out the hair.

6 Place the hair on the head, and to decorate the face make little balls, two black and two green, for the eyes, and a red one for the nose.

7 Varnish the arms and the face with latex varnish mixed with a little bit of water and, when they have dried, attach the face to the arms with glue.

Just attach the figure to a clothes hanger and you're set!

Let your imagination soar

Other ideas:
You can also make a frog, a cloud with the sun, or invent any other amusing decoration.

Mirror

Would you like to make an original frame for your mirror? Follow these steps carefully.

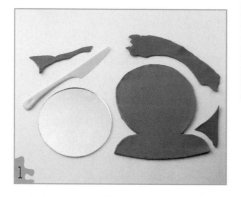

Toolbox

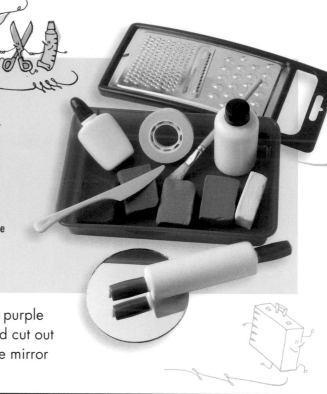

You will need:
- purple, green, white, orange, and red modeling clay
- rolling pin
- plastic knife
- food grater
- round mirror
- glue
- double-sided transparent tape
- latex varnish
- paintbrush

1 Flatten a piece of purple modeling clay and cut out the head using the mirror as a guide.

2 Varnish the head with latex varnish mixed with water, and when it has dried, attach the mirror to it with double-sided transparent tape.

3 Flatten white modeling clay with the rolling pin and place three coils over it, one red, one orange, and one green. Then roll it with the rolling pin.

4 Cut out a bow with the plastic knife and varnish it with latex varnish mixed with water.

118

5 Push the green modeling clay through a food grater to make the hair and varnish the grated pieces.

6 Attach the hair and the bow to the mirror with glue.

Look at yourself in the mirror and...surprise!

Let your imagination soar

Other ideas:
You can also make the entire body of the figure or add a nose in the middle of the frame.

Iris

Following these steps you can create colorful flowers made with modeling clay.

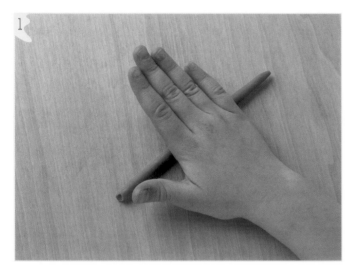

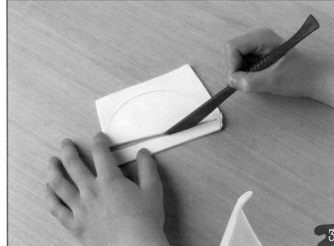

1 Form a coil with light green modeling clay to make the stem of the iris.

2 Make another coil with orange modeling clay, smaller than the previous one, and attach it to one of the ends of the stem.

3 Flatten a piece of white modeling clay with the rolling pin and cut out a half circle.

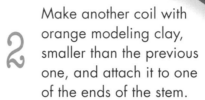

4 Wrap the white half circle around the stem, at the orange end.

Toolbox

You will need:
- light green, dark green, white, and orange modeling clay
- rolling pin
- latex varnish
- paintbrush
- plastic knife

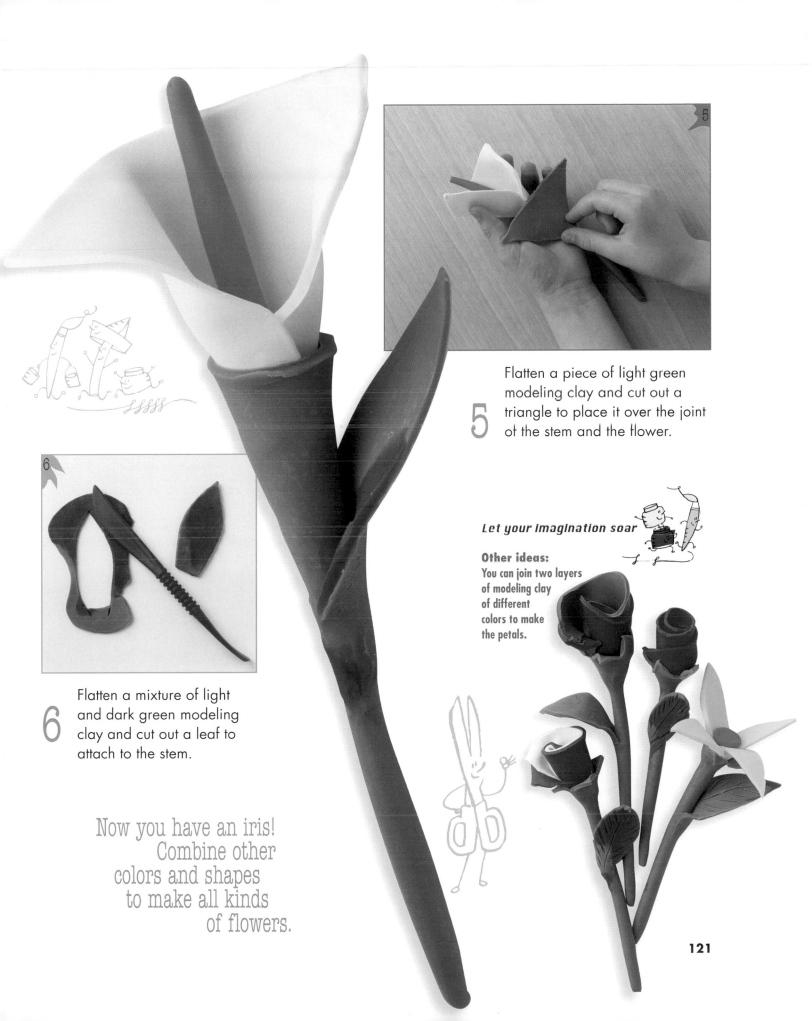

5 Flatten a piece of light green modeling clay and cut out a triangle to place it over the joint of the stem and the flower.

Let your Imagination soar

Other ideas:
You can join two layers of modeling clay of different colors to make the petals.

6 Flatten a mixture of light and dark green modeling clay and cut out a leaf to attach to the stem.

Now you have an iris! Combine other colors and shapes to make all kinds of flowers.

Necklace

Necklace

Necklace

Necklace

Design your own jewelry and show it off with your favorite outfit. Follow these instructions to make it.

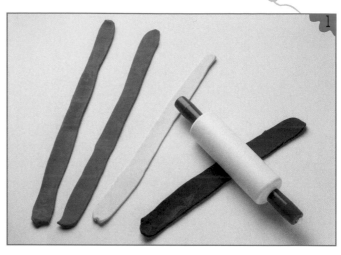

1 Flatten four strips of modeling clay with the rolling pin, one green, one white, one purple, and one orange.

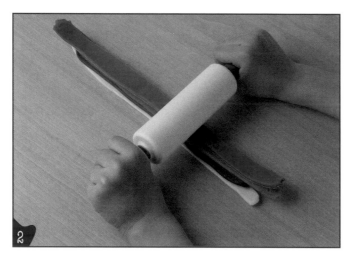

2 Place the strips one on top of the other and press lightly with the rolling pin.

Toolbox

You will need:
- white, purple, green, and orange modeling clay
- orange thread
- large-eyed needle
- rolling pin
- plastic knife
- latex varnish
- paintbrush

3 Cut the four layered strips into a rectangular shape with the plastic knife. Then cut the rectangle into small pieces.

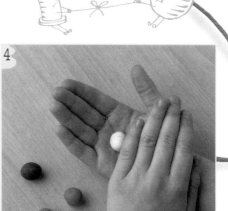

4 Make four balls with modeling clay, one green, one orange, one white, and one purple.

5 Varnish all the pieces with latex varnish mixed with a little bit of water.

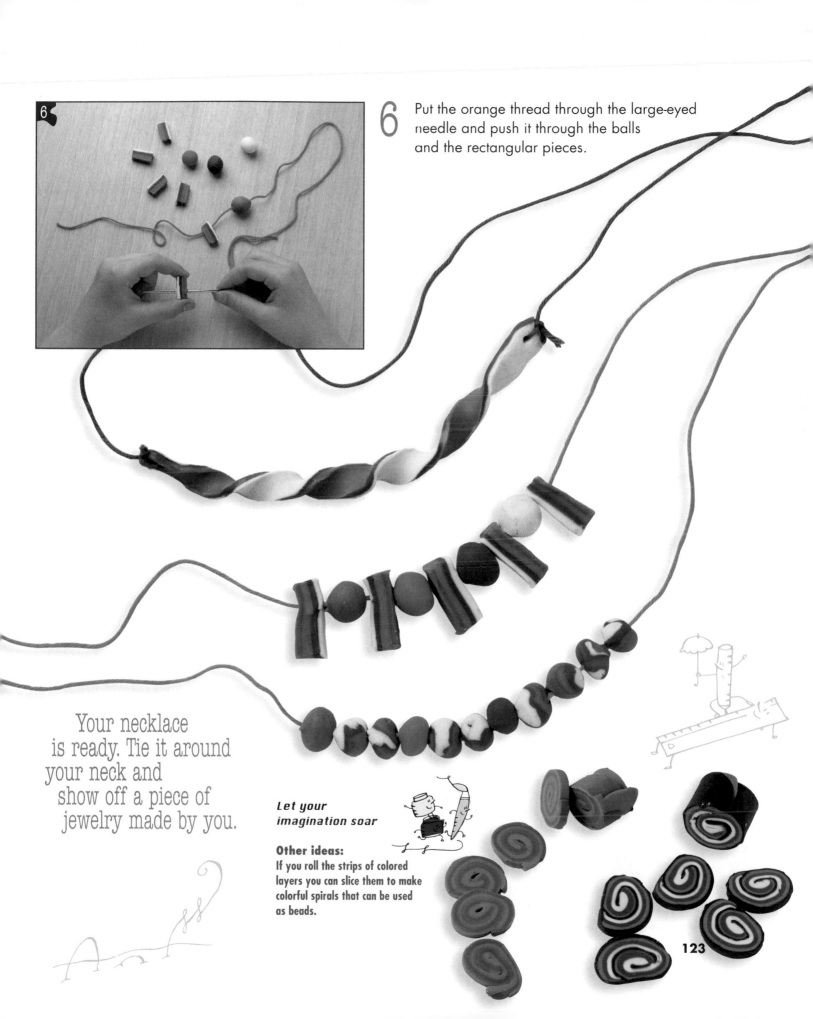

6 Put the orange thread through the large-eyed needle and push it through the balls and the rectangular pieces.

Your necklace is ready. Tie it around your neck and show off a piece of jewelry made by you.

Let your imagination soar

Other ideas:
If you roll the strips of colored layers you can slice them to make colorful spirals that can be used as beads.

123

Plastic

Working with plastic allows you to introduce the concept of recycling and its relationship to the environment. Creating with common plastic objects helps the child become familiar with his or her immediate environment, and to learn at the same time how to transform it. Certain craft projects allow working in groups, which is important in promoting cooperation and working towards a common goal.

Following are some suggestions for making each project, as well as the most appropriate ages for them. It is important to point out that the suggested age, based on the degree of difficulty of the execution of the process, is only to be used as a guide. The projects can be adapted to the level of each group or of each child.

1 **Bubble Monster.** We suggest that each child imagines and draws his or her own monster, in order to promote his or her creativity.
Ages 6 and up

2 **Sun Clock.** This craft can be used to introduce the child to telling time. One can be made for school or for the house.
Ages 5 and up

3 **Basketball Hoop.** Once the hoop has been made it would be good for the child to engage in group play. To do this they can use Styrofoam balls or make them out of cloth, aluminum foil, or newspapers.
Ages 7 and up

4 **Chick Puzzle.** The activity would be more enriching if each child makes a different puzzle so they can later be shared.
Ages 5 and up

5 **Dancing Puppet.** The final goal of this project can be producing a play, so that each child could create his or her own character.
Ages 6 and up

6 **Colorful Flowers.** Plastic planters can be purchased and filled up with sand to "plant" the flowers and to decorate a bedroom or classroom.
Ages 5 and up

7 **Backpack.** This is one of the best craft projects for talking about the idea of reusing an object, thus introducing the theme of recycling.
Ages 6 and up

8 **Binoculars.** This project introduces the technique of sponge painting. They can also be made by younger children if an adult cuts out the bases of the bottles.
Ages 8 and up

9 **A Thousand Faces.** In addition to each child making his or her own, a face can also be made for the entire class by having each child make a piece for the face so its expression can be changed every day.
Ages 5 and up

10 **Pencil Holder Doll.** Through this craft a child can be taught about the need to keep his or her things in order.
Ages 7 and up

11 **Spiders on a String.** A fun activity is to have each child make a spider that will become part of a mobile to hang from the ceiling.
Ages 6 and up

12 **Boat.** If an adult cuts the bottle, this is a project that younger children can also make because it is not very difficult.
Ages 6 and up

Cardboard

Cardboard is a very appropriate material for craft projects, due to the great number of possibilities that it offers. It can be cut, glued, and painted easily with tools found at home. It is important to stress the idea of using everyday things as a basis for making the various projects. This way the child will have the materials to create things at home as well.

Following are some suggestions for making each project, as well as the most appropriate ages for each one. It is important to point out that the suggested age, although based on the degree of difficulty of the process, is only to be used as a guide. The projects can be adapted to the level of each group.

1 **Ping-Pong Paddle.** It is important for each child to make his or her own paddle, to invent a new form or to decorate it with original motifs.
Ages 6 and up

2 **Snail.** To make the project more interesting, snails of different sizes can be made, which can be put together in a mobile.
Ages 5 and up

3 **Parking Garage.** Various materials can be used to decorate the parking garage. Different colored contact paper can be used to decorate it or it can be covered with magazine cut-outs using the *collage* technique.
Ages 7 and up

4 **Flip-Flops.** To make these more durable, a piece of fabric can be used as a substitute for the light, corrugated cardboard, following the same steps.
Ages 6 and up

5 **Camera.** It can also be colored with wax crayons and later painted with a coat of latex varnish.
Ages 7 and up

6 **Ring Toss Game.** One elephant can be made for the class and each child can make his or her own ring.
Ages 6 and up

7 **Pencil Holder.** It is a good idea for each child to invent the shape of the base of the holder, trying it out first with pencil on paper, so it can also be used as a template.
Ages 5 and up

8 **Coin Bank Doll.** It is important for the child to decorate the money bank his or her own way, using the accessories of his or her choice (arms, fabric for covering the tube...)
Ages 6 and up

9 **Drawers.** If an adult makes the templates for the drawers this project can also be recommended for children ages 6 and up.
Ages 8 and up

10 **Balancing Parrot.** Once the parrot is finished, the child, without the help of an adult, should try to balance it, by adding or removing the modeling clay.
Ages 5 and up

11 **Case for Scissors.** This craft can be made at the beginning of the school year so the children can use the case to keep their scissors in throughout the entire year. This way they will realize that they can create useful objects.
Ages 5 and up

12 **Picture Frame.** Following the same steps the children may also frame a drawing made by themselves.
Ages 6 and up

Fabrics

Because the fabrics used in this book are quite common, the child can learn to create using remnants that are found anywhere. Making craft projects with fabrics allows the introduction of sewing techniques. Even then, the projects are designed to be put together in different ways, without necessarily having to use a needle and thread.

1   **Bird.** It is advisable for each child to create and draw his or her own bird in order to stimulate his or her creativity.
    Ages 5 and up

2   **House Shoe-Bag.** To prevent the project from becoming monotonous, some parts of the house can be attached using double-sided tape.
    Ages 7 and up

3   **Braided Doll.** For children 5 or 6 years of age, we suggest making the octopus instead because it is easier.
    Ages 6 and up

4   **Ball.** Wool leggings can also be used instead of stocking material because they may be easier for the little ones to manipulate.
    Ages 5 and up

5   **Car with Trailer.** The most difficult part of this project is drawing the pattern, so an adult should help the children with this task.
    Ages 7 and up

6   **Sock Puppet.** To make this project less complicated, the mouth can be stapled to the sock instead of sewed.
    Ages 7 and up

7   **Organizer.** By substituting a button for the string, the child can be taught to do some basic sewing.
    Ages 6 and up

8   **Yarn Bug.** To make this project more creative, it is a good idea for the child to make several pom-poms and then play at gluing them together to create his or her figure.
    Ages 6 and up

9   **Pajama Pillow.** The older children who already know how to sew can make the pillow with canvas or fabrics.
    Ages 7 and up

10 **Bookmark.** To boost the interest of little children, the theme of the bookmark can be related to one of his or her story books.
    Ages 5 and up

11 **Caterpillar.** To make this a group project, we suggest making a long caterpillar by putting together several different stockings.
    Ages 6 and up

12 **Bag.** For the older children it is preferable to use felt for the strap of the bag, and to sew it at both ends to make it stronger.
    Ages 7 and up

Clay

Modeling clay is a material that is used a lot in schools, and it offers an array of possibilities for crafts.

However, it seems that sometimes it is only reserved for younger children. It is important that children

ages seven and up be aware of the results that can be obtained with this material.

1 **Monkey.** This project is appropriate for ages 5 and up. Any figure can be attached to the rope.
Ages 7 and up

2 **Magnet.** It is not necessary to use the rolling pin. The child can flatten the modeling clay with his or her hand, although the result is never as smooth.
Ages 5 and up

3 **Coaster.** It is best to flatten the modeling clay by hand first to make it easier to roll with the rolling pin.
Ages 6 and up

4 **Let's Eat!** It is best to varnish all the pieces if the child wants to play with them, so they will not lose their shape.
Ages 6 and up

5 **Doll.** Younger children can make any figure. Introduce the technique of using the strainer to make the hair.
Ages 8 and up

6 **Martian Pencil Top.** The heads can be put on drinking straws to make puppets.
Ages 6 and up

7 **Picture Clipboard.** If wood is not available, this painting can also be made using cardboard for a base.
Ages 5 and up

8 **Astronaut.** A mobile can be made with planets of different sizes and colors by adding pieces of wire.
Ages 6 and up

9 **Clothes Hanger Decoration.** It is not essential to use the rolling pin. The figures can be formed by flattening them by hand on top of the table and attaching them to the clothes hanger.
Ages 5 and up

10 **Mirror.** This project may be easier if the mirror is attached with double-sided transparent tape to a piece of wood or cardboard.
Ages 7 and up

11 **Iris.** The stem of the flower can be a piece of wire covered with modeling clay and varnished, so it can be bent.
Ages 6 and up

12 **Necklace.** It is important to varnish the pieces before they are threaded to prevent them from losing their shape.
Ages 7 and up